THE CHURCH AND CHILD SEXUAL ABUSE

WESTERN THEOLOGICAL INSTITUTE

The Church and Child Sexual Abuse

TOWARDS A PASTORAL RESPONSE

Edited by
Eamonn Conway, Eugene Duffy
and Attracta Shields

the columba press

First published in 1999 by
the columba press
55A Spruce Avenue, Stillorgan Industrial Park,
Blackrock, Co Dublin

Cover by Bill Bolger
Origination by The Columba Press
Printed in Ireland by Colour Books Ltd, Dublin

ISBN 1 85607 279 7

This is the second in a series of pastoral resources produced by the Western Theological Institute.
The first is *Celebrating the Triduum,* edited by Eugene Duffy and Enda Lyons, 1999, published by The Columba Press.

Copyright © 1999, The Contributors

Contents

Introduction	7
Child Sexual Abuse: A Systemic Approach 　*Attracta Shields*	11
Beyond the Myths: Child Sexual Abuse by Females 　*Attracta Shields*	21
An Invitation to Wounded Healers: 　*Reflections of a Victim of Sexual Abuse*	35
In Hope of a Better Day: The Perspective of those who have Sexually Abused Children 　*Attracta Shields*	42
In the Front Line: Who cares for the Carers? 　*Colm Healy*	47
'Do you want to be well again?' 　*Alan Hilliard*	53
The Dilemma of those in authority 　*Colm O'Reilly*	61
Forgiveness and Reconciliation in the context of Child Sexual Abuse 　*Eugene Duffy*	67
The Service of a Different Kingdom: Child Sexual Abuse and the Response of the Church 　*Eamonn Conway*	76
Western Theological Institute: Vision Statement	91
The Contributors	93

Introduction

Survivors of the crime of Child Sexual Abuse know how healing it is to be able to tell their story. A new climate of openness and accountability has given many victims the courage to do just that, to confront those who have abused them, regardless of their position in society.

This new climate is largely the result of investigative journalism that has faced down the power of society's hitherto most trusted institutions. However, investigative journalism and media have a dynamic and rhythm of their own. They have led us to the truth, but not always to the whole truth.

This collection of essays is an attempt to stand back not from the pain but from the dramatic headlines, to move from knee-jerk reaction to considered response. The reader will note two kinds of contributions, pieces written from personal experience and reflection, and analysis by psychologists and theologians.

A victim of sexual abuse by a priest shares with us her own personal journey of recovery and self-discovery. Motivated by her desire to help those currently in pastoral ministry, she helps us to understand the wider implications of abuse for home and family life.

Colm Healy, who directs a residential childcare service, also considers the number of people indirectly effected by child abuse. He outlines what it is like when a colleague at work is accused of Child Sexual Abuse and outlines practical suggestions for the protection both of children and childcare workers.

Alan Hilliard, a Dublin priest, describes a similar experience in a church context. He reflects on the reality of working in parish ministry in a diocese where a number of fellow priests have been convicted of Child Sexual Abuse. He also critiques the church's handling of such situations on the ground and calls for more support for those in the front line.

Those in charge, however, always face a dilemma. Bishop Colm O'Reilly puts a human face on those in authority who have been the subject of much criticism but who nonetheless struggle to balance justice with compassion both for victim and offender.

As a chartered psychologist, Attracta Shields has wide experience of counselling both those who have been abused and those who have abused. Her postgraduate studies in London and in America have also provided her with an opportunity to research the causes of Child Sexual Abuse at an international level and attempt to separate myth from fact. She presents here a systemic approach to the problem that is grounded both in science and in philosophy. She also invites reflection on two issues seldom considered: the perspective of the offender, and women who have abused.

Even in the face of the most heinous cases of sexual abuse, the church must still work to bring about healing, forgiveness and reconciliation. Such work can easily be misunderstood as an attempt to cover up, to try to forget and move on without really acknowledging the hurt and dealing with the damage. The likelihood of misunderstanding is compounded when the abuse has occurred within the church's own ranks. Acknowledging that this is a highly emotive area, Eugene Duffy's contribution tries to balance the sensibilities of the victim with the gospel demand to forgive sin. Writing as a theologian, he also challenges the church to take a prophetic stand in defence of the dignity both of victim and offender, regardless of what is popular in wider society.

The challenge to the church is taken up in another theological contribution by Eamonn Conway, who argues that the experience of Child Sexual Abuse by priests raises fundamental questions about the way in which power and authority are exercised within the church. He also claims that priest offenders are scapegoated in an effort to avoid addressing these more basic issues.

Finally, he argues that the church must be humble enough to allow itself to be brought back to its original mission by the victims of sexual abuse, many of whom still look to the church for healing.

Child Sexual Abuse is the polar opposite of what priests and religious are meant to be doing. It is understandable, therefore, that those in authority in the church took some time to accept the reality that a small number of their fellow workers had committed this crime. Sadly, but again perhaps understandably, the first aid sought was from the legal profession. Dealing with priests and religious facing criminal charges was foreign and frightening territory and legal expertise was required. Initially at least, pastoral considerations and responsibilities took second place. This book represents an effort to redress an imbalance and to bring pastoral perspectives to the foreground. It challenges the church to consider fully the demands of the gospel, and take a courageous stand to uphold the dignity both of victim and of offender. The book also challenges society to look behind the headlines, to consider its own complicity in creating a climate which colluded with sexual abuse in the past, and which is still reluctant to act responsibly towards victim and offender. It challenges all people to consider their own responsibility for creating a society in which sexuality is respected as a gift and lived out responsibly.

The Western Theological Institute, Galway, has commissioned the papers in this volume.

Eamonn Conway
Eugene Duffy
Attracta Shields
Galway, October 1999

Child Sexual Abuse:
A Systemic Approach

Attracta Shields

Introduction
During a seminar some years ago I first heard the French phrase *'reculer pour mieux sauter'* which can be translated as 'stepping back in order to leap forward'. This suggests maintaining a non-dogmatic stance regarding issues that are in an evolutionary process of discovery. I believe that this idea of stepping back in order to leap forward is most apt when considering the whole subject of Child Sexual Abuse. This is an area that is still clouded by myths, contradictions and confusion. There are many opinions on this subject. However, it is necessary to continue to research all aspects of this phenomenon and to continue to inform ourselves to ensure that we are not in any way inadvertently contributing to the maintenance of the cycle of abuse.

The problem of Child Sexual Abuse is systemic since it affects the person who has been abused, the person who abuses and all those people in the systems they inhabit – family, spouses, medical personnel, legal personnel, counsellors, to name but a few.

From a systemic perspective, the focus is on the reciprocity of relationships. For example, if something happens that affects one member of a family, it affects the entire family, whose response, in turn, affects that individual. This suggests that any behaviour must be studied in the context in which it occurs and not in isolation. If I for one moment reflect on even one person with whom I have worked who has been abused, a host of other people whose lives have also been affected by this abuse clamour for attention. Heidegger illustrates very well our interconnectedness with other people and the world when he refers to the human person as Being-In-The-World-With-Others.[1] The hyphens indicate that this is a unitary concept, which indicates our involvement with other people and with our environment. This concept is important when dealing with Child Sexual Abuse, since there is some evidence which seems to suggest that assumptions on the part of parents, professionals, or society in general regarding the nature of abuse and their reaction to it, can impede rather than facilitate the person's management of the situation.

What follows is an attempt to analyse a range of issues which have dominated the debate so far, in an attempt to begin to formulate a response which will take account of the unique nature of each individual case, while at the same time balancing it with competence in tried and tested methods of intervention. To this end I will draw mainly on my own clinical experience and research and contemporary research evidence. The privilege of listening to the many stories of my clients, the challenging questions posed by my colleagues, students and other interested people together with the ever growing research material, have, over the years, highlighted for me that information about Child Sexual Abuse continues to unfold. It is indeed a multifaceted complex problem, which requires a multidisciplinary response.

Child Sexual Abuse defined
The term 'Child Sexual Abuse' has entered into our vocabulary with extraordinary familiarity, with most of us assuming that we know what it means. It might, however, be useful for us to ask ourselves the question 'How have I acquired my knowledge?' For many people most of their information on this subject comes from the media. A study of the commercials on television pinpoints the fact that the media presents us with consistent and stereotypical messages with regard to male and female roles, interests and personality characteristics. These messages also abound in most advertising media as well as in literature, films, drama, and many other aspects of society.

While the literature abounds with definitions of Child Sexual

Abuse it is problematic because of the varying attitudes towards it. Since the definitions are so varied they may lead to some confusion. There is, however, some agreement that any involvement of dependent, developmentally immature children in any sexual activity that they do not fully understand, or that is inappropriate to their age and level of development, may be termed abuse. The inequality in the relationship between the adult and the child, and the child's level of development, renders informed consent impossible.

Ferguson and Mullen[2] point out that there is a tendency in the literature to reify Child Sexual Abuse as though it were a specific syndrome, like measles, that can be recognised by the presence of a grouping of invariant symptoms that occur together. However, there are no objective signs and symptoms that can define Child Sexual Abuse; it depends rather on normative data for definition. Evidence is collected usually from retrospective self-reporting about childhood sexual experiences, and this data is then evaluated against normative standards to determine whether or not the reported experience can be classified as abuse. Those classified as having been sexually abused form a very heterogeneous population, with abuse occurring in varying combinations, intensities and durations. This heterogeneity regarding the definition of Child Sexual Abuse poses problems for estimating the prevalence of this problem, since these estimates may be reduced by including only those cases of severe intrusive incidents, or they may be inflated by including incidents which were non-physical and non-intrusive.

It is more beneficial to take each type of potentially harmful sexual experience to which children are exposed and determine the extent to which this experience has damaging effects for them. There is, therefore, a movement away from defining Child Sexual Abuse in a way that reifies it as a specific syndrome, towards descriptions that focus on the nature, intrusiveness and extent of the sexual experiences in childhood and how these experiences may affect children and adults.[3]

Theories of Child Sexual Abuse

In an effort to explain Child Sexual Abuse, some theoretical perspectives have been proposed. One such perspective draws heavily on psychoanalytic theory and, more particularly, on Freud's writings on infantile sexuality and the Oedipus complex (which refers to the boy's unconscious wish to get rid of his father and to be alone with his mother, and the girl's view of herself as her mother's rival for her father's love). For quite some time this theory was used to focus on the 'seductive child' and the 'pathological mother', or to dismiss reports of incest as infantile fantasy.[4] Freud proposed a direct causal link between sexual traumas experienced in childhood and later adult neurosis. Later, Freud retracted this theory and proposed that the stories of sexual trauma in childhood, that he heard from his patients, were fantasy.[5] This theory of childhood fantasy of seduction dominated the psychiatric literature until the 1960s. Therefore, in psychiatric literature, it was claimed that incest was a rare phenomenon, even though reports of it may be common, and that where it did occur it was the result of the child acting out her desire for her father. The psychiatric literature also indicated a 'pathological' mother as an explanation for father-daughter incest. Many instances in the literature suggest that sexual abuse is instigated by the mother's abandonment of husband and daughter. This theory has been strongly criticised on the grounds that it shifts the blame onto the child or the mother. While psychiatry has revised and corrected many of its concepts concerning Child Sexual Abuse, most particularly the tenet that it is a rare phenomenon, this has not been accompanied by satisfactory research to correct some of the assumptions and myths surrounding the causes of abuse.

Another widely used explanation of sexual abuse is the notion of the 'dysfunctional family'. The mother is viewed to be dysfunctional since she fails to meet her husband's sexual demands and fails to give adequate nurturance to her children. In the dysfunctional family system the daughter appears to have responsibility for childcare, housework, etc., together with her

A SYSTEMIC APPROACH

sexual duties towards her father. The family dysfunction concept regards 'pathological family relationships (cold distant mother, infantile father, love-starved daughter) as the (main) issue while the actual occurrence of incest is a secondary manifestation, a symptom. Incest is treated in some of the literature as a functional system serving to hold together a family whose internal relationships are so abnormal as to be otherwise completely unstable.'[6] The family dysfunction theory focuses on the mother and daughter while omitting the father's position. In a somewhat stereotypical manner, the right of the father to have his sexual and nurturance needs met by females is not questioned. It is only a problem when he demands his needs from his daughter rather than from his wife.

The Power Theory is a theoretical framework used by workers at Dympna House in Sydney, a centre for persons who have been abused. It is now also the method of approach in many other such treatment centres. The power theory provides a framework that includes socio-political factors, familial factors and individual characteristics, and thus provides the basis for a comprehensive approach to Child Sexual Abuse. The theory uses two concepts of power: *structural* power, which is power over others, and *personal* power which is power within oneself. Structural power is 'the power granted to individuals or classes of individuals by society'. Child Sexual Abuse represents a misuse of the power, the power that society 'legitimately accords particularly to males'.[7] Personal power is the power that resides within the person. For some individuals this personal power is well developed, healthy and positive, while for others it is underdeveloped, distorted or neglected. Thus it may be harmful to themselves and to others. Some individuals who have a strong personal power may, however, operate from a base rooted in fears and anger, rather than self-worth and an appreciation of the worth of others.[8]

The Power Theory challenges the stereotyping of traditional sex roles for males and females which redresses the power imbalance and thus reduces the risk of inequalities. This poses a challenge to a patriarchal system that can result in the exploitation of children and those who are physically weaker. It is important to understand that stereotypes are the products of fear, a fear that often comes from a lack of knowledge of the facts. It is necessary to understand these issues in order to create the climate for the safe nurturing of children, where Child Sexual Abuse is unthinkable. However, much more work and research is needed to achieve this ideal since change is slow and difficult, largely because of the losses involved in relinquishing power and privilege.

According to some of the research available to date, there is some evidence to suggest that power is a factor that can be closely linked to sexual abuse. Galbraith suggests three types of power situations: *Condign power* he attributes to the person who secures the submission of others to his or her own purposes by threatening punishment if the other refuses to comply; *compensatory power* refers to the person who offers a reward in order to achieve compliance from the other person; whereas, with *conditional power* it is through education, social beliefs and persuasion that the person becomes disposed to submit to the will of others.[9] Therefore, when we refer to power in relation to sexual abuse, we see that it is a complex and multifaceted issue.

Power is a creative and God-given gift, which each person receives and which is necessary to maintain a healthy level of mental health. However, some individuals, in an effort to avoid existential anxiety and a certain level of uncertainty and insecurity that are an inevitable part of human existence, seek to inauthentically build false 'securities'. This they do by creating structures that dominate and control others to achieve their ends. Such structures as the unequal power relationships between men and women, that are perpetuated by institutions and ideologies, create a climate for abuse of power. Thus any such unhealthy climate provides the milieu where Child Sexual Abuse is likely to occur. It is, therefore, incumbent on all of us to be aware of the possible ways in which we as individuals may seek to control others and thus abuse our power. It is also the responsibility of each one of us to work to challenge unjust structures, which seek to dominate and control and abuse power.

The person who has been abused

In spite of all the care and concern and the efforts made to understand Child Sexual Abuse, the easiest thing to do in working with children is to lose sight of the child's perspective. This is understandable since the child's view opens up a frightening and unpredictable world. It necessitates using one's own feelings to understand what it must be like to be abused and to feel powerless to alter the situation. Ten years ago I suggested that this may be one of the reasons why most of the literature focused on causation. Now, ten years later, we are only beginning to give attention to the impact of Child Sexual Abuse on children, with most of the research still focused on the effects of abuse in later life. From my experience there is little doubt that children exposed to sexual abuse find it a very distressing and confusing experience. The inequality between a child and adult is sufficient to forewarn of emotional problems, and the physical problems due to the difference in size and strength present clear-cut medical hazards.[10]

Ferguson and Mullen suggest 'that the majority of studies that have compared children known to be sexually abused with non-abused control participants have found higher rates of adjustment problems among the abused children, with these problems spanning mental health symptoms, low self-esteem, and problem behaviours including aggression, delinquency and sexualised behaviour.'[11]

A symptom which is sometimes observed in children who have been sexually abused is over-sexualised behaviour, which includes sexual overtures towards adults or other children, as well as compulsive masturbation and sexualised body language.[12] This may be understood in a behavioural sense as a form of learned behaviour, from repeated abuse over a period of time. There is, however, a gap in the theory, since there is no conscious memory in the child's mind of the sexualised behaviour having been learned. It is important to note, in working with children who have been sexually abused, that they can act out parallel behaviour in a diagnostic interview. I have found that, on occasion, as children describe the manner in which they have been touched by an adult, they may at the same time be touching themselves. When the behaviour is pointed out and interpreted as something that may have happened to them, they are unembarrassed and show that they are unaware of what they are doing. Children who are treated while they are still young, respond very well to treatment and there is an end to their sexualised behaviour usually in a short time. It is more difficult to achieve similar results with children who are older and who have been exposed to sexual abuse over a prolonged period.

The fact that a child engages in a wide range of fantasies, including sexual fantasies, in no way implies that the child wishes to have sexual contact with an adult. Clinical evidence suggests the importance of taking into account the role of physiological arousal in children who have been sexually abused. This means that these children can become aroused and excited by the sexual experience and can experience pleasure. The consequences of this may result in the child dissociating from the experience and having a sense of intense guilt. On the other hand, the child may expcrience the abuse as a grossly unpleasant and uncomfortable experience. In this case response to the abuse may result in a clinical profile similar to post-traumatic stress disorder, where repression of the conscious memory of the abuse is replaced by the development of bodily symptoms.[12]

One of the long-term consequences of childhood sexual abuse can be the disruption of normal and social development. The way in which each person responds to abuse is unique. Not all who have experienced sexual abuse in childhood are damaged. However, for those who experience difficulties, help is available and they can recover.

Towards the formulation of a response
We need to change some of the language of the sexual abuse system. For example, the term 'victim' conjures up an image of a helpless, hopeless person and this can affect how a person internalises this image of himself or herself. Similarly, the label 'sur-

vivor' can portray an image of a person who is just surviving rather than moving on to live a full and fruitful life.

We need to challenge the system, which continues to maintain the myths around sexual abuse. There is resistance, even on the part of many professionals, to acknowledge that theory, research and clinical experience still leave us with many questions. Knowledge and understanding of the subject of Child Sexual Abuse is, as yet, at a very elementary stage. Due to the complexity of the issues, there is a danger of focusing attention and resources totally on the past to the detriment of confronting the present situation. A proactive stance is vital to prevent Child Sexual Abuse, rather than concentrating solely on dealing with the effects. It is necessary to provide people with knowledge based on sound research data. An integrated educative process is needed which facilitates an understanding of sexuality and develops a healthy approach to the development of the whole person.

We need to put in place processes which will help each one understand the interconnected nature of the whole of our society and how each part influences every other part.

We need to continue to explore the cultural factors that are at work which create a climate in which power can be abused. An analysis of society's response to Child Sexual Abuse could provide some useful information regarding the norms of our society. If these norms can be explored in a multifaceted, integrated way, a much stronger sense of healthy societal norms can be developed.

Conclusion

No stone must be left unturned to put an end to Child Sexual Abuse, which inflicts so much pain and suffering on the lives of so many people. It is a wonderful privilege to work with so many people who succeed in turning their lives around and move on to live creative and fulfilled lives. However, I look forward to the day when we can live in a collaborative way where respect, equality and justice prevails and sexual abuse will not be possible. To arrive at this day will require hard work and sound research together with the participation of all systems within our society. I have hope that, with commitment from all relevant sources, we can do it.

Notes:
1. Heidegger, *Being and Time*, Oxford: Blackwell, 1988.
2. David M. Ferguson and Paul E. Mullen, *Child Sexual Abuse*, London: Sage Publications Inc., 1999.
3. Ibid.
4. E. Driver and A. Droisen, *Child Sexual Abuse*, London: Macmillan Ltd., 1989.
5. S. Freud, *Three Essays on the Theory of Sexuality*, London, 1962.
6. Driver and Droisen, op. cit.
7. Ibid., p. 102.
8. Ibid.
9. J. Galbraith, *The Anatomy of Power*, Boston: Houghton Mifflin, 1983.
10. F. Rush, *The Best Kept Secret, Sexual Abuse of Children*, New York: McGraw-Hill Book Company, 1980.
11. Ferguson and Mullen, op. cit.
12. F. Vizard, 'Child Sexual Abuse – the Child's Experience'. *British Journal of Psychotherapy*, Autumn, 1988.

Beyond the Myths:
Child Sexual Abuse by Females

Attracta Shields

Introduction
Those of us concerned with Child Sexual Abuse are travelling along a continually evolving journey towards understanding the facts and their many multifaceted underlying issues. Over the years clinicians and researchers have been trying to uncover the layers of this phenomenon in an effort to discover effective ways of responding to the complexities of abuse and its far reaching effects on the lives of so many in our society.

In a paper which I wrote on Child Sexual Abuse in 1989, based on research in the USA, Canada and Britain, the conclusion was that Child Sexual Abuse is a major problem, that the offender is overwhelmingly male, that the victim is almost exclusively female, that about 80% of the time he is a family relative or friend of the family of the person abused, that actually incidents are grossly under reported and that offender behaviour crosses all social, economic and racial boundaries.[1]

During the 1980s and the early 1990s in Ireland much work was done in actively presenting Child Sexual Abuse to professionals, policymakers and the public in general as sufficiently prevalent and damaging to demand an immediate response.

The features which first dominated the dissemination of knowledge regarding Child Sexual Abuse implied that a substantial number of females were victims and that assaults were committed predominantly by males. As more males are coming forward to report incidents of Child Sexual Abuse, it is becoming apparent that a sizeable number of males have been sexually abused as children. In addition to this there is an increasing number of male and female clients reporting Child Sexual Abuse by females.

From the research literature that abounds, which is attempting to clarify issues relating to Child Sexual Abuse, there are some obvious lacunae. The subject of female sexual abuse of children still remains a relatively unexplored issue. The fact that, to date, it appears that females constitute a minority of those who sexually abuse children is not an excuse for ignoring this problem. If we do not understand the problem, it is even more difficult to respond with appropriate solutions. There is a great reluctance to address the issue of sexual abuse by women because of the fear that it may detract from the greater and more pervasive problem of abuse by males. However, if a climate is to be created that can effectively deal with all forms of Child Sexual Abuse then it is necessary to confront the issue of abuse by women. This paper sets out to investigate psychologically some aspects of female Child Sexual Abuse and assess its effects on those who have been abused. It will also explore some implications for the nature of a response. To this end, I will draw on my experience of working with women and men who have been sexually abused by women, women who have sexually abused, and research evidence available to date.

Sexual abuse, socialisation and sex-role stereotyping
Child Sexual Abuse occurs within a social and cultural context. It is necessary, therefore, to research and examine the context in order to understand the nature of environments which predispose the establishment of abusive behaviour patterns. Socialisation has a marked influence on how we might view abuse and how we respond to it. Socialisation begins at birth and is the integrating process which enables the child to become a full member of society. It includes all the influences that make one an accepted member of society and helps one to establish and maintain relationships with others.

For more than a century a controversy has raged in professional spheres over the relative contributions of heredity ('nature') and environment ('nurture') to the course of human development. Today, most psychologists agree not only that nature and nurture play important roles in development but that they interact continuously to shape it. Therefore, the development of many personality traits appears to be influenced almost equally by heredity and environment.

Sex-role behaviours, therefore, are multi-determined. There is an interplay of biological, psychological and social factors affecting the development of gender identity. Gender refers to the characteristics associated with masculinity and femininity. These characteristics vary over time and can differ in different cultures and societies. Despite the efforts of many women and men, and despite the focus on social justice which seeks to eliminate the many forms of oppression such as sexism, racism, class distinction and so on, still many Western women and men have been socialised to conform to sex-role stereotypes in relation to many issues, including how they view and handle their sexuality. Throughout history, patriarchy and hierarchy have had a profound influence on the socialisation and sex-role stereotyping of Western women and men, affecting their experience of sexuality, anger, psychological maturation and many other aspects of life.[2]

Patriarchy is a social system of male dominance based on assumptions of male superiority, which is reinforced by social institutions such as the state, the church, the family and education system. Patriarchy refers to a form of institutionalised dominance. Its cornerstone is the distinction of what it is to be a man or a woman. It underpins many of the attitudes and values of society. Starkey says that patriarchy is 'another name for the power structure of the state, the school, the home, the financial empires, the armed forces, the law courts'. 'It is echoed in almost all human societies and belief systems; in Islam and Marxism as well as Catholicism and Capitalism.' 'What is more, patriarchy is not affected by having a few women in top decision-making jobs. Most women who occupy such posts themselves accept and reinforce patriarchy by the decisions they have made, because in order to have reached such a position in a male-dominant society they needed to internalise patriarchal values ur they themselves become token men.'[3]

From a psychological perspective, it is clear that such a system breeds violence, rejection, powerlessness and oppression, which creates an environment conducive to many forms of abuse, including Child Sexual Abuse. Given the complex nature of this type of system and the difficulty of the theoretical and research issues involved, it is clear that no quick solutions for Child Sexual Abuse are at hand. Much psychological research suggests that for a person to become an oppressor they must have first experienced some form of oppression.

Many cognitively alert and socially attuned men and women are aware of the progressive decline of the patriarchal system and resist attempts by various institutions to maintain its structures. This is a positive step forward since women, and to a lesser extent men, have been the object of strong and persistent stereotypes. The dimension of aggression-passivity became the norm for sex-role differentiation. For the most part, sex-role behaviours are perceived to be related to aggression in some way. Men were assumed to have such desirable traits as rationality, decisiveness, confidence, independence and ambition. Women, on the other hand, were seen to have such traits as passivity, dependence, submissiveness, emotionality and indecisiveness. Men were seen as strong and 'macho' while women were seen as mothering, nurturing and caring.

On analysis of the media, the manner in which systematic and consistent images of masculinity and femininity are portrayed is astonishing. For the most part we are unaware of the way in which we profoundly internalise cultural stereotypes. Because these stereotypes are persistently reinforced, we come to view them as 'natural' and universal rather than as merely one expression of human possibilities.

Sex-role stereotyping has many negative effects. Men and women have unrealistic expectations of themselves and set goals that are unattainable. This sets individuals up for failure, which leads to frustration and very often a poor self-image. Restricted stereotypical views of masculinity and femininity confine the resources of both men and women. Women are prevented from expressing the stronger aspects of their nature, while men cannot access their emotional and nurturing qualities. Rather than fostering complementarity, this sets up competition not only between women and men but also between women and women and men and men.[4]

Therefore, women and men are very often confronted with expectations of how they must behave and act within a competitive and often aggressive society in a way that does not concur with the beliefs and values with which they can live comfortably. To curtail the freedom of people to fulfill their full potential and express their uniqueness and diversity creates a climate that justifies the victimisation of anyone who is different or weaker.

Sexual abuse and attitudes towards sexuality
The prevailing attitudes and values in society deeply influence how people symbolise sex, love and power. The evidence available to date seems to suggest that Child Sexual Abuse thrives in a culture where sexual gratification is viewed as a right and where violence and abuse of power is either an implicit or explicit social norm.[5] Despite the fact that there is some progress in talking about sexual matters, we can hardly say we live in a culture that has healthy attitudes to sex. In general, sex and sexuality have been treated as matters of top secrecy. It is for each person to ask himself or herself how naturally, comfortably and helpfully he or she can talk about his or her sexuality. Our culture provides little opportunity for women and men to develop healthy, integrated sexuality. 'The sexual terrain of our times is filled with fear, uncertainty and reactivity.'[6] This is evidenced by the response to Child Sexual Abuse, which is clouded by myths, misinformation, scapegoating, denial and many defensive reactions.

The language sometimes used with children, such as 'private parts', 'parts nobody else should touch' and so on, suggests the genitalisation of human sexuality. The consequences of this can lead to very unhealthy attitudes towards sexuality. It is reminiscent of dualism, which drove a wedge between 'body' and 'soul', 'flesh' and 'spirit'. It suggests a suspicion and distrust of the body and sex, and 'sets the body, sensuality and sexuality against the holy, the pure and the spiritual'.[7] When the body is disassociated from the total person (the self) it becomes objectified. This in turn leads to the objectification of sexual behaviour and of sexual partners.[8] An adult or child who is seen as an object is an easy target for sexual or other forms of abuse.

Patrick Cannes[9] talks about various themes that adversely affect our sexual lives. We are all familiar with the proliferation of women's and men's magazines offering advice on how to achieve control and get our needs met in our relationship with the opposite sex. This suggests competition and manipulation rather than mutuality and loving. Books such as *Men are from Mars, Women are from Venus* are bestsellers and an indication of peoples' feelings of ambivalence and anxiety about sexuality. Traumatic sex is also prevalent in our culture. This is evidenced by the number of television shows and news media stories that portray an obsession with issues of sexual abuse, violence and sexual and other forms of exploitation. The media played an important role in raising awareness of Child Sexual Abuse and other forms of injustice, but the continued portrayal of sex and violence with sexism embedded in it can lead to misinformation, misunderstanding and negative messages about sexuality which amount to a form of social abuse. On asking a reporter why the media is almost obsessed in presenting incidents involving violence, sexual deviance and Child Sexual Abuse, he did not defend it in the name of freedom of speech or people's right to information. Rather his reply was, 'This is what our people appear to want to hear about.' Regardless of how we interpret these stories, there must be some parts of them which resonate with some aspects of our internalised experiences.

Fear of our sexual vulnerability frequently expresses itself as anger. Both men and women have been socialised to believe that there are reasons for fear in their relationships with each other. They translate this fear into anger. Since anger is not considered to be a socially acceptable emotion by many people, it is denied and repressed. This can lead to enormous subconscious conflict in relationships between men and women. The result of fear and anger leads to competition, compulsions and dualism.

Competition is the quest for power. Psychologists suggest that the root of competition lies in the need to use power and control as a defence against fear, anxiety and feelings of inadequacy. Psychiatrist Karen Horney suggests that competition is a problem for all of us. It is necessary, therefore, to be aware of this and to take steps to move towards more collaborative relationships. This requires recognition of the equality of men and women and an acknowledgement of their complementarity. Many people are compulsive about being in control. This blocks listening and the ability to form mutual healthy relationships. The focus for the compulsively competitive person is to control self and others. To avoid the acting out of the desire to control, both men and women must listen to each other and accept each other as equal partners in a relationship.

Dualism is a way of viewing life in terms of polarities or either/or categories, e.g. body-soul, good-evil, male-female. The insidiousness of dualism lies in the fact that one pole of the dualistic dichotomy is considered good or superior while the other is bad or inferior. When maleness and femaleness are viewed dualistically, it pigeonholes men and women into a competitive mode of relating. Therefore, in a relationship a man may seek to dominate in an effort to have control, while a woman may use indirect manipulation or seductiveness to gain some sense of power and control. If we face the truth, we will come to realise the reality of the oneness, unity and interconnectedness of all creation. It requires both men and women to develop self-awareness, self-acceptance and self-honesty![10]

There have been mixed reactions to the introduction of the 'relationship and sexual education programme' in primary schools. Some parents are totally opposed to the introduction of this programme. They suggest that sex education is the parents' responsibility, yet many of these same parents report that there is frequently little or no talk about sexual matters in the home. Some teachers too resist participating in this programme. This is understandable and points to the fact that there is a need for a widespread education programme for both adults and children. This programme would enable all people to understand the nature of human development and the full complexity of what it is to be a human person with potentialities as well as limitations. It would enable people to understand their sexual nature, feelings, behaviours and inclinations and thus develop the capacity to relate comfortably to men, women and children in an emotionally mature way. This may be the first step on the road to gaining some further understanding of the context in which it is possible for any person, be they male or female, to sexually abuse children.

Prevalence of female sexual abuse
Research in the past few years shows that an increasing number of men and women are reporting that they were sexually abused as children by their babysitters, their mothers, their aunts, their grandmothers or other females. Since the majority of reported sexual offences against children are committed by males, little attention has been given to the issue of female sexual abuse. Therefore, any data on this topic is tentative and the studies available give some inconsistent and conflicting information. Dr Fred Mathews, at a conference given in Toronto in 1991, states that 10% of those who sexually abuse children are females.[11] Just as in the case of male sexual abuse, it is very difficult to get accurate figures because of the different definitions of sexual abuse, the population samples from which the data are drawn, the approach and methodologies used to assess the prevalence of abuse, and other confounding factors such as sampling error. One consequence of the studies done is to highlight the fact that Child Sexual Abuse is a major problem. However, when it comes to presenting accurate statistics, great caution must be exercised.

Recent studies investigating Child Sexual Abuse of males revealed that a minority of those who abuse are females. Some obvious differences emerge when one looks at the gender of those who are abused. The rate of male offenders has been found to be as high as 97.5% (weighted average) when the person abused is female. However, when the person abused is male, the weighted average estimates falls to 78.7% for males which suggest 21.3% perpetration rate for females.[12]

Kathryn Jennings, in her review of the literature on females who sexually abuse, cautions of the possibility of sexual abuse by females being grossly under reported.[13]

Females who sexually abuse children: Under reporting and denial
Deeply embedded in our culture in the Western world is the view of women as nurturing and caring, thus rendering it impossible to believe that any woman could possibly have the capacity to abuse a child. However, I have had men and women, albeit small in numbers, who have reported childhood sexual abuse by women. Ten years ago at a conference, when I referred to sexual abuse by a woman the response was one of shock, horror and disbelief. The general remarks were, 'How could a woman abuse? It could not be possible, it could not be proved.' We have just moved slightly from this position. However, the taboo and secrecy around the issue of Child Sexual Abuse is slowly being eroded as more evidence becomes available.

There is research to illustrate the lengths to which individuals will go to conform to strongly held social norms. It is not surprising, then, that the issue of female Child Sexual Abuse is so vehemently denied. The theory of dissonance argues that human persons seek to eliminate inconsistency between their attitudes or inconsistency between their attitude and their behaviour.[14] The defence of denial is one way of reducing dissonance. The gender biases we hold obscure issues relating to sexual abuse by females.

There is a focus in the literature on males abusing females, therefore it is more difficult for those who have been abused by women to report it. Since there is such secrecy and taboo around the subject of sexual abuse by females, those who have been abused feel very isolated and often believe that they are alone in their experience. They sometimes doubt that they may be imagining it or that it is just a dream or a fantasy. While, in the US, support groups for those who have been abused by women have begun over the past few years, nevertheless, many of them find their stories of sexual abuse discounted.[15]

Boys experience particular isolation when they are sexually abused by a woman because any sexual contact between boys and older women is rarely regarded as abuse. Indeed, in some cultures, sexual activity between a younger boy and an older woman is looked on as a conquest for the boy and something that initiates him into manhood. This in no way minimises the seriousness of the offence. It leads to great confusion for the child and any reporting of it is met with disbelief.[16] Some researchers present possible explanations as to why males may not report abuse by females. It is more difficult to find evidence of sexual abuse by females. The socialisation process, which portrays women as caring and nurturing, is a barrier to acknowledging sexual abuse by women. There may be embarrassment on the part of adult males to disclose sexual activity with their mothers or other females. Because of the lack of awareness of professionals or others regarding abuse by females, this aspect of abuse can easily be overlooked. Due to the formerly held belief that abuse of males rarely affected them, their reports of abuse were often ignored.[17]

Females too have difficulty reporting childhood sexual abuse by women because it challenges the stereotypical view of women as nurturing and caring and therefore incapable of abuse. Women are viewed as the passive recipients of sexuality, rather than as the initiators, a view which renders it difficult to imagine a woman sexually abusing others.[18]

Characteristics of females who sexually abuse children
It is important to emphasise that data on the characteristics of females who sexually abuse children is based on a handful of studies and very limited experiences in this area. From the data

available to date about females who sexually abuse children, it appears that they are a somewhat heterogeneous group.[19] Some studies suggest that women who sexually abuse have significant problems in functioning, and high rates of mental illness and of substance abuse. However, cautious conclusions must be drawn from such studies. It may be that females who sexually abuse children must be ill or disturbed to be recognised by professionals as offenders.[19] There is also some evidence to suggest that sex-role stereotyping leads to a higher rate of diagnosis of mental disorder for females. A diagnosis of mental disorder for women who engage in Child Sexual Abuse may be employed to eliminate the cognitive dissonance resulting from such behaviour which contradicts social norms.

It is not possible to describe the 'typical' female who sexually abuses. One can, however, look at some general information that is available. Females who abuse are usually close relatives or friends of the children they abuse. They engage in a variety of sexual acts. These involve fondling, mutual masturbation, oral, anal and genital activities, the use of enemas and sexual games. Many women who sexually abuse appear to have low self-esteem and are dependent on men for their sense of identity. From the evidence available, it appears that many females who sexually abuse also abuse alcohol and/or drugs. Some of the women who abuse were themselves abused as children. Some females abuse independently while others abuse in cohort with another person (usually a male).[20]

Why might females sexually abuse children?
The reason why females abuse is unknown. There are, however, some tentative attempts to explain what is, as yet, relatively unexplored territory.

Although women may feel powerless outside the home, this structured powerlessness of women in the public arena may be translated into a state of total control in the home. There is some evidence to suggest that Child Sexual Abuse may be the woman's means of achieving control in a powerless situation.

However, over concentration on the power theory may only address one side of the equation. Women who were themselves sexually abused may have cognitive impairment, which results in distorted thought processes and identification with their abuser.

The expectations of women to be nurturers and carers can create internal conflict when their impulses are not congruent with the external norms. In an effort to resolve this conflict they may engage in violent activity.[21]

Child Sexual Abuse may indicate arrested psychosexual development and emotional immaturity. Women thus seek relationships with children with whom they can identify. Drug or alcohol abuse may act as a disinhibitor and thus lead to Child Sexual Abuse.

Effects on those who are sexually abused by females
Because of the strong attachment bond between a child and his or her mother, abuse by a mother may make the individuation process more difficult. Part of the normal process of child development is the separation from parents and the establishing of their own identity as autonomous individuals. There is a blurring of boundaries for children who have been sexually abused by their parents and this inhibits their normal individuation process. Women who have been sexually abused by a woman may experience maturation difficulties and anxiety around their developing bodies. They may engage in childlike behaviour in a defensive effort to remain as children. They have ambiguous feelings towards their mother who abuses them. They repress their anger since they fear that this may totally separate them from their mother. However, this anger must be confronted and worked through so as to avoid it being turned in on themselves. Unresolved anger can lead to bitterness and feelings of revenge.

The boy who is sexually abused by his mother will experience great conflict. Because of his socialisation process, if he has pleasurable feelings he will believe that he was not abused. If he does not experience pleasure, he will experience shame and guilt. Boys who have been sexually abused by women are likely to repress memories of the abuse. When these memories are recovered, they can have an extremely disturbing effect.

Some pointers for the way forward
It is necessary to realise that some changes in our society are necessary. Change only occurs if the system changes. Our response so far is too narrowly focused, disjointed and defensive. It is not a matter of pitting one discipline against the other. What is required is a multidisciplinary approach, so that, rather than addressing the symptoms, we can focus on the underlying problems.

Child protection is of primary importance as is care for all those who have been affected by abuse. However, it is also necessary to address the needs of children in the future and also the needs of adults. There is an indication from research in the UK that too intense a focus on child protection can lead to a neglect of the wider needs of both adults and children. There is a need to commit resources to full scale integrated research, which will point the direction for the elimination of this problem from our society. It is necessary to provide an integrated education programme for both adults and children, which will lead to a healthy understanding of masculinity and femininity. Education will also involve an understanding of life span development and a socialisation process that will engender equality and collaboration between men and women.

Conclusion
It is clear that the sexual abuse of children by females raises a plethora of questions for which there are, as yet, no answers. I realise the limited scope of this paper, the many issues that have not been addressed and, indeed, the many issues that have not, as yet, been recognised. However, if it inspires further debate, some on-going research, and puts pressure on the government to commit resources to move toward a solution of this issue, then it will have achieved its aim.

Notes:

1. F. Rush, *The Best Kept Secret, Sexual Abuse of Children,* New York: McGraw-Hill Book Company, 1980.
2. Janet Malone, *Gender Differences in Handling Conflict,* Human Development Vol. 14 (1), Spring 1993.
3. *Social Science,* Unit 8, p 124, Milton Keynes: Open University.
4. Baron and Byrne, *Social Psychology,* Boston: Allyn and Bacon, 1994.
5. Mike Lew, *Victims No Longer,* London: Cedar, 1998.
6. Patrick Carnes, *Sexual Anorexia,* Hazelden, 1997.
7. Mary Elizabeth Kenel, 'A Celibate's Sexuality and Intimacy', *Human Development,* Vol. 7 (1), 1986.
8. Hollida Wakefield and Ralph Underwager, *Return of the Furies: An Investigation into Recovered Memory Therapy,* Chicago: Open Court, 1994.
9. Patrick Carnes, op. cit.
10. Catherine Casey, 'Women and Men Collaborating in Ministry', *Human Development,* Vol II (4), Winter 1986.
11. Kathryn J. Jennings, 'Female Child Molesters: A Review of the Literature' in *Female Sexual Abuse,* Michelle Elliott (ed.), New York: The Guildford Press.
12. David M. Ferguson and Paul F. Mullen, *Child Sexual Abuse,* London: Sage Publications, 1999.
13. Kathryn J. Jennings, op. cit.
14. Baron and Byrne, op. cit.
15. Ellen Bass and Laura Davis, *The Courage to Heal,* London: Vermillon, 1996.
16. Mike Lew, *Victims No Longer,* London: Cedar, 1993.
17. Kathryn J. Jennings, op. cit.
18. Ibid.
19. Ibid.
20. Ibid.
21. Olive Wolfers, 'The Paradox of Women Who Sexually Abuse Children' in *Female Sexual Abuse,* op. cit.

An Invitation to Wounded Healers: Reflections of a Victim of Sexual Abuse

Introduction
I agreed to write this paper because I wish to influence the pastoral response of priests and bishops to victims of Child Sexual Abuse. I am myself a victim of sexual abuse. I also have some experience in pastoral ministry. In what follows I wish first of all to share my story, and then, briefly, by way of conclusion, its implications for pastoral ministry. I do so in order to encourage priests and bishops to engage in the only kind of ministry which can prove life-giving and healing, a ministry that comes from the very depths of life itself.

My story
I was born the first child of four. My mother nearly died at my birth. Later, one brother and two sisters joined me; there were two years between each of us. When I was born I weighed just two pounds. I understand that my Dad did not look for me for two days. When he eventually did, he found me in a drawer wrapped in cotton wool.

At seven years of age I was back in hospital to have part of a lung removed. A strange thing began to happen at that time: it was then I started to mind my Mam. When I went to the hospital to see the doctor I watched her every move and noticed what her reaction was. This went on for three years as I was brought in and out of hospital. I did not like the doctors. I do not remember Mam ever saying, 'You will be all right'. I often felt she was annoyed with me for being sick. Once while in hospital a child died in the ward. When I stood up in my bed to see what was happening, I was told to lie down and be quiet. No discussion took place – this I found very frightening and I remember it to this day.

I made my First Holy Communion when I was eight years of age, on my own, as I was in hospital when all my classmates made theirs. I was very nervous. I felt Mam was too. I missed a lot of Primary School due to illness and hated this. I felt different. I had to wear lots of clothes which were too long for me but which were put on me to keep me warm because I was so sick. 'You would not be able to ...' was the phrase I heard most during these years.

Confirmation was another frightening experience. As I remember it, the church was locked behind us and we trembled in case the bishop would ask us a question. If we missed it, so we were led to believe, we would not be allowed to make our confirmation. Even then I wondered if this was how Jesus had meant it to be.

When I went to Secondary School I was still a very nervous person. In order to develop my self-confidence, the nun put me in charge of ringing the bell. I think it helped. When we reached our teenage years Mam could not cope with us – she was very cross and threw tantrums and objects at us. We had a terrible fear of her. I spent a lot of time under the table playing, or lying in bed for safety. A few times I remember calling for Dad to save us, but he was always working or out in the shed. I think he was also afraid of Mam.

Like most schools, we had school retreats and I remember longing to have a chat with one priest who came in. I wanted to talk to him about home and about growing up but I lacked the courage. A friend later introduced me to another priest who had given us some retreats and was a friend of hers. I went to see him a few times. As trust built up, I began to tell him my feelings of fear, my non-understanding of life, and my puzzlement about sexuality.

He then abused me. My trust turned to fear. I do not remember leaving the room that day. I closed down and did not tell anyone. I was now left only with my fears and my mistrust, which had spread to mistrust and fear of everyone.

I was in the Legion of Mary and in the choir. These were the only ways I could get out of the house. My Mam liked me doing all these 'good' things. Through this I thought I could gain her affection and score some 'brownie points'. This went on for years.

At 21 years of age I joined a convent. There was a priest there as chaplain but I was afraid of him in case he would turn out to be like the other one. I stayed in the convent for six months, and then, thank God, I came out. I know now that entering religious life was another thing I did to make Mam like me. I remember that the chaplain who brought me home also took me for a short drive in his car. I felt very uncomfortable indeed.

Next I went to work in a hospital as a medical secretary. This I really enjoyed. However, I still felt lonely and needed someone to talk to. Loneliness, as we all know, is one of life's most painful human wounds. 'A person can keep his sanity and stay alive as long as there is at least one other person who is waiting for him', according to Nouwen. In search of companionship, I joined the scout movement as a leader. This enabled me to get into my 'busy mode' again. I didn't have much time to think. I was doing some good. I was getting people to like me for what I did for them.

During this time I met a man whom I did not like very much. However, I remember that at Easter he bought me an Easter Egg, a really expensive one. He arrived with it to the door. Thank God, my Mam was not in. I just took the egg and said thank you. I put it under the bed so that Mam would not see it and I gave it to her for Easter. She was very pleased and thought I was great.

When I was 24 years of age I met my future husband. We had a hard time when he came to the house. Mam would have tantrums. She would huff and puff a lot, and even on occasion, throw milk bottles. I remember asking him how he could marry me with a Mam like that. He said that he was not marrying her and that he loved me. I will never forget that day – it was great. Eventually, we got engaged. There was no great excitement in my house but I do remember Mam asking me, 'Are you sure you will be able for marriage? You know, he will not be around all the time and you might be on your own.' I nearly changed my mind but I did not. It took me a long time to realise that my husband loved me for being me because when you are used to people misusing love and pretending to love, it is very hard to regain trust in anyone. To be honest, these are issues we are still working on as a couple.

We got married and two years later we had our own house quite near Mam's. This was important to me because I still needed to mind her and look out for her. I went on to have two children, the best thing that ever happened to me. Through them I learned the meaning of unconditional love. I have always loved them to bits even when they sometimes disappoint. And if that is how I love them, I can only imagine how God loves us. My love for them has taught me all I need to know about God's love.

We went down to Mam's every Christmas for dinner because my brother and sisters had also left home and I could not bear to think of my parents being on their own. It was a nightmare for me because Mam would not let me help her. My husband was great and very understanding and the children never noticed anything wrong. They loved their granny and she loved them. In the evening we would go for tea to my husband's home. In contrast, there was a great atmosphere there. We worked hard at keeping everyone happy. Each year I had asked Mam to come to our house for Christmas dinner. In the last year of her life, to my surprise, she said 'Yes'. It was the best Christmas of my life – I bought new tablecloths, candles, etc. And it was a great day – very peaceful and I was in control. It was Mam's last Christmas.

The next chapter of my life began when I did a course in lay ministry, which was recommended by a priest friend of mine. It was during this course that I heard for the first time, that 'the glory of God is a human being fully alive'. I said to myself, 'I am not alive.' I asked myself, 'What does this mean?'

Later that year I was chaplain at a youth summer camp during which a girl was sexually abused. I had to listen to her story and meet with the police and her parents. It was an extraordinary moment in my life. I happened to be there for her. I walked with her in her great hour of need. I remember her parents thanking me for being there for her, for being so understanding, and remarking that this had helped her to cope. Later, I got very upset. Memories of my own abuse came back. I became angry. Why did I never have anyone to walk with me in my hour of need? I wanted to tell someone, but whom could I trust? Each time I tried to tell, it did not work out. This reinforced in me a sense that I was to blame for the abuse that had happened to me. But I was determined to talk to somebody. I really prayed, maybe for the first time in my life. I cried out, 'Jesus prove to me that you care. Send me someone who will understand me – that is all that I ask.' He did.

I went to this friend who was a priest and, on the third attempt, in a few spluttered words, I told him of my abuse. I thought that my heart would burst. I cried. He gave me a glass of brandy and thanked God for being there. I never felt so close to Jesus as I did that day. That was the first day of my resurrection and of becoming fully alive.

I became more relaxed and trusting as my story began to unfold. My experience with this priest was so different. From him I received the healing pastoral care I so much needed. Then during these weeks, Mam died suddenly in the operating theatre in hospital. She died on her own. It was terrible. At the funeral my brother kissed Mam in the coffin and said that this was the first time he had kissed her that she did not push him away. Talking a few months later as a family, we acknowledged for the first time that we had all been hurt because of Mam's non-affection and cold nature.

Sometimes, for example, I have wondered if my sister only married her husband to get free of Mam. As it happened, Mam liked him, as he was the son of a neighbour whom she also liked and had known as a child. When my sister brought another lad home, Mam threw tantrums. For the sake of peace, my sister went back to the first lad and married him. It has been a very difficult marriage. My other sister never married. She could not relax. She could not bring home lads she liked and instead used to meet them at the corner. As a family we still grieve for what never was in our lives because of the way Mam was, but we are happy that at last she is free and at peace.

A few months after Mam's death, relations we had never met before came to tell us chapters of Mam's life story that she had kept hidden from us. What we heard was terrible. She was an only child whose mother had died having another baby. Her father married the maternity nurse who never took to Mam, and from birth her life went simply from bad to worse. We realise now that Mam acted towards us in the only way she knew how. Now, for the first time, we feel close to her and we believe that she is helping us now in a way she was not able to up until after her death.

Coincidentally, the day Mam was buried I received my certificate in lay ministry, and during the ceremony I felt her closer to me than she had ever been in life. The first time I ever gave a public talk was last year on my birthday, and I felt that she had given me a new life on the same day that she had given birth to me. It was very emotional. Recently I received another qualification, this time a diploma in counselling. It took place on the fourth anniversary of Mam's death. I never got to tell her of my abuse and hurts, but now I believe she knows all and is there for me.

My journey of personal healing has continued. I have received pastoral care from other priests and church people that have come to know of my abuse. I have contacted *Faoiseamh*, a helpline established by the Conference of Religious of Ireland for people such as me. In due course they referred me to a professional psychotherapist who is also a priest. His counselling has given me deep healing, strength, hope, peace and confidence in my life today and for the future. I now believe in myself and do not worry so much about protecting others or wanting to change them. I realise that the only person I can change is myself. That is what I have done and what I am still working on.

AN INVITATION TO WOUNDED HEALERS 41

Pastoral ministry in the light of my experience
My personal story has taught me much about the kind of ministry that can bring Christ to people, and the kind of ministry that is doomed from the beginning. By way of conclusion, I wish to point a direction for the kind of ministry I believe will genuinely help people to recognise God in their lives.

I know that, at its best, pastoral ministry involves a deep human encounter in which people are willing to put their own faith and doubt, hope and despair, light and darkness, at the disposal of others. In this way they help others to find a way through their confusion and reach the solid core of life. The very element that is most personal and unique in each one of us, if only we had the courage to share it, is probably that which would speak most deeply to others. It is the nature of things that we heal others through our wounds. We are 'wounded healers', as Henri Nouwen puts it.

By entering into communion with human suffering, by sharing with others our own painful struggles, we give relief and we experience relief ourselves. We are all tempted to cling to who we are and what we have. Christian hope frees us to move away from safe but arid oases and enter unknown and fearful territory. My hope is that the church will listen and learn to walk with people on their journey and thus heal the whole body of the church before more limbs fall off.

In Hope of a Better Day: The Perspective of those who have Sexually Abused Children

Attracta Shields

Introduction
I have worked both with people who have been abused and those who have abused, and I care deeply about all those people whose stories and painful journeys I have been privileged to share. In this paper, I would like to share with you some of my experiences of working with people who have sexually abused children. I acknowledge that engaging in sexual activity with children is, without any doubt, abusive and in most cases deeply distressing and damaging.

My primary goal in writing this paper is to help you to understand that these people are human persons like you and me. They can confront, work through and change their abusive behaviour. They can develop compassion and empathy for those they have abused. They can grow and develop and strive to live life in a way that is worthwhile for themselves and others. I am touched by their strength and courage, and, in spite of what they have done, their ability to live out their humanity. For those of you who have been sexually abused, I can well understand that you may be extremely angry with the person who abused you and you may not, in any way, want to understand any person who has abused. This is fine for you. I fully understand that the healing process is unique for each person and it is not possible to rush or abort it.

Confronting and owning their sex-offending past
The first step for the person who has abused is to accept responsibility for their wrongdoing towards innocent young persons

whom they have abused. This includes coming to an awareness of the hurt (much of which may be on-going) they have caused to those they have abused and to their families. Likewise, it involves being conscious of the pain that their abuse has caused to their own family, friends and colleagues. They become deeply aware of the many people who suffer because they have broken the trust they had in them. They experience feelings of deep remorse and revulsion for what they have done. They come to a stage of having a sense of helplessness that they cannot turn back the clock and undo the hurt and distress they have caused the young people they have abused. They acknowledge that all who have been hurt are deserving of a heart-felt apology and an expression of deep remorse.

During a time of great trauma there is a tendency for the dark patch to take over the entire canvas of the person's life. The trauma becomes internalised and tends to obliterate all the good inherent in the person's life. This experience can be true both for the person who has been abused and the person who abuses. The person who has been abused may at first see no immediate hope for healing and may experience themselves as bad, with the episodes of abuse covering over all the good in their life. The path to recovery for the person who has been abused involves the painful and sometimes slow process of coming to realise the truth about his or her innocent role in the abuse, the letting go of the internalised abuse and the reclaiming of his or her inherent goodness. The remorseful person who has abused may experience the dark side of his life as so powerfully shameful that he believes it has placed him beyond redemption in the eyes of society and the eyes of God. The road to recovery for the person who abuses requires a major confrontation of the wrong in his life, and engagement in a process which will enable him to turn away from offending. This turning away requires a realisation that, despite the evil in his life, there is also goodness and it is vital that he reclaims this goodness.

The man who abuses: What is he like?
The lives of those who abuse are for the most part quite ordinary lives until the time of their offending. They are considered to be good citizens in their locality. They are often sensitive, charismatic, and talented. A tiny minority may be controlling. Many of them have deep spiritual values. They mostly have a limited understanding of their sexuality. They often have a rigid sense of their sexuality and it is sometimes linked to a rigid moral standard. In many cases, people who abuse are very successful in most areas of their lives. However, they have unresolved sexual issues, which remain unexplored and unresolved. These issues eventually express themselves in some way and they find their expression in the form of sexual abuse. It is not clear why the person abuses, and those who abuse continue to question themselves as to why their otherwise good life took the turn in the direction of abusing. It is difficult to pinpoint any particular moment or event in the lives of these people that could be seen as a causal link to their abusing sexually.

The nature of the abuse
The essential nature of sexual abuse involves oral/genital contact, sexual fondling, or any sexual intrusion of the child's body, as well as sexual intercourse in some instances.

Society's response to the person who offends
If we are to take our cue from the media and from the reaction of many people in our society, the response is predominantly hostile towards the offender. He is labelled and scapegoated and the mentality in general is that he should be locked up and the key thrown away.

Whenever we experience fear or anxiety, we displace it onto persons or objects that are not the real origin of these anxieties. We live in a society where we do not have a healthy positive attitude towards our sexuality. We are also, at some level, aware of our potential to be exploitative, manipulative or abusive in our relationships with others. Sexual offenders, therefore, become the scapegoats for our own anxieties around our sexuality and our potential to abuse. The greater our anxiety the more we will attempt to disassociate from it. Thus, we will demonise sexual offenders to make them more unlike ourselves so that we can distance ourselves from that which we cannot accept in ourselves. We label all sexual offenders as paedophiles, which refers to only a small minority of those who sexually abuse. Paedophilia is 'the act or fantasy of engaging in sexual activity with prepubertal children as a repeatedly preferred or exclusive method of achieving sexual excitement'.[1] This is a psychosexual disorder and most sexual acts with children do not warrant a diagnosis of paedophilia.

Clerics who sexually abuse children
Clerics who sexually abuse children are not at all as numerous as we are led to believe by the 'high profiling' media attention which they receive. Likewise, there is constant gossip, which is the forerunner of scapegoating, of 'the raft of upcoming cases'. Few clerical sex charges are contested in the courts. One wonders if it is possible for a cleric to get a fair trial in the present climate. Clerics who have abused, and indeed others too, have engaged in useful therapy in the long run up to their trial and sentencing. Prison sentences break that pattern of curative therapy and can set it back years. Clerics who sexually abuse often feel uncared for and isolated from the church. The priests against whom allegations are made are removed from their parishes and, with loss of home and friends, experience unbelievable grief. While the church, in its framework document for a response to Child Sexual Abuse, attempts to address the issue, much more is required if all persons – those who have abused and those who have been abused and all those who have been affected by abuse – are to be facilitated in working towards recovery and fullness of life. Wounds are everywhere, but 'suffering becomes meaning-generating or redemptive when it leads to reflection, interiority and most importantly compassion'.[2] The church must be at the forefront of the process of healing.

It is necessary for the church to address, as a matter of great urgency, the issue of what happens to the cleric who is released from prison after serving a sentence for Child Sexual Abuse.

Conclusion

From my experience, most of the men who sexually abuse, when they work through their process of confronting their abuse, come to an awareness of themselves and grow spiritually as they develop deeper capacities for truth. It is heartening to see them develop a care for themselves and others, which exemplifies a living of the compassion of Christ.

It is important that more informed approaches be taken toward all those who sexually offend. The whole issue must be placed in its proper context. The person who has offended is a human person who has engaged in abusive behaviour, but who is also inherently good. It is impossible to help any person if we do not first recognise inherent goodness in spite of their wrongdoing. This in no way excuses the wrongdoing, nor does it allow the person to evade his responsibility for what he has done. The offending behaviour calls for curative/rehabilitation measures. Prison is not the place for rehabilitation and it is necessary to move into a space in our understanding where prison is not seen as the place to deal properly with sex-offending. Non-custodial sentences, with the emphasis on on-going therapy, would, no doubt, prove to be much more effective. Healing and spiritual renewal occurs when we place our trust in God who loves us unconditionally.

Notes:
1. American Psychiatric Association, *Diagnostic and Statistical Manual of Mental Disorders*, (4th edition), Washington D.C., 1994.
2. Robert Grant, *The Way of the Wound,* 1121 Juanita Ave., Buklingame, California 94011, USA, personal publication.

In the Front Line:
Who cares for the Carers?

Colm Healy

Introduction
This article assesses yet another dimension of the impact of Child Sexual Abuse. It explores what happens when an allegation of sexual abuse is made against a fellow care worker. I say 'allegation' because in my experience the initial effect of an allegation and the fear of an allegation can impact on carers just as much as an actual incident of abuse. It can be many weeks or months before an allegation is shown to be false or true. This can be a most difficult time.

The people involved
I will begin with the impact on myself. I arrive into work and someone tells me that an allegation has been made. Immediate reaction: numbness, fear, and confusion. An allegation. Against whom? Who made it? Even before I have the details, the first thing I must cope with are my feelings. In a care setting, particularly where the children are residential, life must go on. There is often very little time to dwell on one's own feelings – yet what can happen if I don't handle them appropriately?

Next my mind turns to the colleague against whom the allegation has been made. How do I feel towards him? He is a team member, perhaps a friend, certainly someone I trusted. Could it be true? What or whom do I believe?

Then there is the child who made the allegation. This is a child whom I know, whom I like, with whom I work. Perhaps a disturbed child, one prone to telling lies on occasion. But is this a reason not to believe him or her? As a professional, I know and accept totally that a child comes into care to be protected and to be safe. This child needs support and help, regardless of the truth of the allegations. And it is my job to give it. Yet this child has just turned my life and the life of my friends upside down. Of course, I might believe the child totally, but even here I must be very careful if I'm to give appropriate support to the child.

And what about the rest of the care team? They are experiencing the same range of thoughts and feelings, if even in a different order. One can imagine what this does to the atmosphere in the workplace!

It is no ordinary workplace, however. It is a children's home. If an allegation can cause so much upset to a group of adults, it can be all the more upsetting to the other children. How much should they be told? How much do they know already? How much can different individuals cope with? Some of these children will already be victims of abuse. How much has the child who made the allegation told them? The children often know more than the staff because they have talked together. How do they understand what has happened? What do they believe? Children who have been hurt in the past and need to feel safe and protected are now living in a house full of doubt, fear, blame, and uncertainty. At a time when staff need care themselves, they are required to be more caring than ever.

There are still more people who are affected. I go home after work to family and friends. What can I say to them? Very little – yet they are asking questions as to why I am not my usual self. If the media get involved, how do I handle it? As among the clergy, the crimes of convicted care-workers have not done a lot for the self-esteem of the rest of us. Now I'm going to have to listen to jibes and comments and particularly misinformed judgements. I may ignore them but I will still feel hurt by them.

Finally, I will have to deal with those called in to investigate the incident. Gardaí, Health Board officials, solicitors. This means interviews and examination of work practices. It means trying to remember accurately incidents that may have happened ages ago.

WHO CARES FOR THE CARERS?

The effect on childcare centres and childcare as a profession
Those at the front line of care must withstand the first painful onslaught of an allegation. However, children, adults and whole families can be deeply disturbed when an allegation is made, especially in a small residential childcare facility. It is not surprising, therefore, to discover that where an allegation of Child Sexual Abuse has been sustained, often residential homes do not survive. Where an allegation has been shown to be false, it can take a long time for the wounds to heal. In some cases they don't heal; it effects their work forever. It is understandable that anyone who has witnessed or experienced the effects of an allegation will look to their own situation. This can be good if it leads to better practice. However, it may also lead to workers backing off from children, not being prepared to take normal risks, not getting close, not trusting, refusing to be alone with a child – you can draw your own conclusion as to how this impacts on the quality of care the children might receive.

Children need good role models, yet it is getting more difficult to get men involved in childcare. Many have left the profession rather than risk losing their reputation through a false allegation. Others, because of financial commitments or whatever, stay in the workplace and feel trapped and ineffective as carers.

What is the impact on the individual against whom an allegation has been made? If the allegation is substantiated, then they must take responsibility for their actions. But if the allegation is shown to be false, how do they put their lives back together again? What, as so often happens, if the result of the investigation are inconclusive?

Strategies for improvement
It would be very wrong of me to move from this depressing and stressful situation without pointing out that it does not need to be as bad as I have painted. There are two key questions which, if addressed, could at the very least reduce the negative impact of Child Sexual Abuse on the caring profession. These are: What will help me cope if an allegation is made against a colleague or

myself? And how do I reduce the possibility of a false allegation being made?

Long before allegations are made, we need to learn how to deal with them. People who work in the front line of care must have a network of support in place at all times. This includes regular team meetings, attendance at training sessions, involvement in interest groups, active membership of professional bodies, e.g. The Irish Association of Care Workers (IACW) or The Irish Association of Pastoral Formators. Most important of all is a relationship with a good professional supervisor. This is someone who knows and understands our work and with whom we can be open and non-defensive. This person can guide us in our work and be there for us if something goes wrong. The 'Lone Ranger' mentality is a liability to all of us. We have to struggle to overcome it.

It is also important to have agreed guidelines in the workplace in the event of an allegation. These should include directives on who will be responsible for conducting an investigation and the procedures that must be followed. All those involved, the alleged victim, the accused, colleagues, children, have a right to know what support they can expect. It is important that this is all written down, because in a stressful situation things and people can be overlooked.

Through personal supervision and our network of support we will hopefully grow in self-awareness. This sensitivity to ourselves will help us in crisis situations and also help us to be sensitive to how others are being affected. I believe we owe it to the children as much as to ourselves that we lessen the possibility of false allegations. My first suggestion is to have a clear set of Safe Practice Rules. They do not need to be restricting or to prevent the spontaneity that can be so valuable in caring for children. In my own work, a simple rule that says I must let a colleague know where I am going to be and for how long, if I'm working with an individual child, is a valuable protection for myself and the child. My co-worker can casually check that all is well from time to time. This is much better than not being alone at all with a child.

I also recommend open communication with co-workers. It is important to belong to a supportive team, in which we can give and accept feedback without being defensive. Child protection is everyone's responsibility. The saying 'the harder the thing to tell, the greater the friend who tells it' is very relevant here.

Lastly, being in touch with ourselves, our feelings, our sexuality is very important. If in the course of our work we feel uncomfortable with our own responses or actions or those of others, we should use our support network to talk about it. It may be scary but it is better that we get out of a dangerous situation before harm is done.

Conclusion
Finally, it is only natural that a group of caring people, whose ethos is steeped in the Christian message, would see a need to show compassion to the offender. Many offenders are victims of abuse themselves. While they, as adults, must accept responsibility for what they have done, it is in everyone's interest that they do not offend again.

I would like to suggest that our response to victims should also be guided by our Christianity. It seems to me that too much advice has been taken from lawyers and not enough from the gospel. The fear of litigation has overshadowed the desire to be involved in the healing process. If we really understand how Child Sexual Abuse can turn a person's life upside down, we will also realise that many victims are looking for no more than to be believed with trust and acceptance. If this is given in a suspicious and begrudging manner, then our one opportunity to take part in the healing process is lost. I've no doubt that the church will be 'ripped off' by a few people as a result of such trust, but is that really the church's problem? For many, a large part of the healing process is to confront their abuser or the symbol of their abusers (the church). It is the 'being listened to', 'being believed', 'being accepted', 'being trusted' 'being seen as a good person' and being 'apologised to' in a sincere and personal way, that will re-empower the hurt child – even if that child now lives within an adult body. The empowered child can forgive and let go. I feel strongly that the church's response to Child Sexual Abuse is very much a matter of faith.

'Do you want to be well again?'

Alan Hilliard

Part of the problem

'You guys are the cause of all these problems, but you are also part of the solution.' Very profound words from a victim of clerical sexual abuse. They were spoken to me when the storm was at its worst. As with most people, I didn't know where I stood. At times I was defensive of the church. At times I was angry and resentful of it. At times I blamed individuals. At times I just collapsed with a profound sense of morbidity and disillusionment.

That phrase stayed with me. 'You are part of the problem – but you are also part of the solution.' Why didn't this person just leave the institution that did so much damage? I could understand and even absolve such a gesture. It was creating more problems and questions for me. If she had just gone on the attack, I would have closed the door and said, 'Who could blame her?' Trying to make me aware that I was part of the solution was placing a responsibility on me that I could do without.

I know a number of people who are victims of clerical sexual abuse. Many of them are not interested in compensation but are interested in the future of their church. They have discovered their need of God in their journey. Their faith is important to them. They need to be listened to, accepted and reassured that their voices are heard. They desire to make the church a place of compassion and care, a church that accepts the errors of its way. Due to fear, victims are at times painted with the one brush. Yet many of them have a richness and depth in their observations and comments that are inspiring and touching. They teach us about forgiveness and compassion in ways most real.

In this paper I was asked to look at the effects of the climate of abuse on the organisation that I am a part of, the church. I am looking at this from my perspective.

Let me begin by stating the truth. We have had to admit as a church that members of our organisation sexually and physically abused minors. The actions that were taken when these crimes came to light were at times inappropriate and shortsighted. I could sum up the atmosphere in the wake of these revelations like this:

Talk about loss of confidence.

Comments passed on the street.

Fear of wearing clerical dress.

Feeling under suspicion in the presence of nephews and nieces.

A lack of inspirational leadership.

In other words, there was a lot of confusion and turmoil. There were few to offer hope in the midst of the chaos. So, with the aid of a few like-minded friends, one could stumble through. Some members of the organisation may have been more directly affected because they either knew some of the offenders or they shared accommodation or shared a ministry with them. In these cases fellow clergy, who didn't experience the effects of abuse at such a deep level, couldn't understand the hurt. Among one's own one felt isolated. To help us in our chaos, experts were drafted in. They filled us with theories, told funny stories, guidelines were written. This is similar to the Keynesian theory that the rising tide will lift all boats. Once our heads were put in order, all would be well. But our hearts were still in our boots. Wounded, battered and, in some cases, tramped upon, we were talked at, not listened to. And if listened to, there was very little feed-back.

Then there is the issue of the organisation. I need do no more than refer to the survey that was undertaken in Dublin and which was published in April 1997. The two greatest sources of stress for the priests of Dublin were general church leadership and clergy scandals. At the same time there was a marked decline in the number of candidates for priesthood as well as many resignations from active ministry. Sadly, nobody asked why.

The fact was the organisation had lost its confidence. For a long period priests felt their voices couldn't or shouldn't be heard. Their sense of self as an organisation was very low. Every statement was measured against the experience of having lost their moral authority. Berated by (some not all) elements of the media, we felt like children left in the corner of a school room. We wanted to get back into the life of the classroom again but were helpless as to how we should go about doing it.

John Hunt, in his *Managing People at Work,* has listed the most commonly found behaviours that can limit, inhibit and block the work of groups:

- Restricting information. The answers are known but can't be told. 'For legal reasons'.
- Lying. Deliberate distortion of the facts in order to preserve a position in the group.
- Pairing. Breaking into sub-groups rather than solving the problems together. Responding to the immediate rather than looking at the overall objectives of the process.
- Fighting. Win and dash; loose conflicts within the group. *Una Voce.*
- Flight. Withdrawal. Can be physical (holidays or retreats), psychological, or symbolic (depression, sulking, sleeping, doodling, telephoning).
- Noise. Speaking to be heard rather than contribute.
- Suppressing emotion. Demanding logic and rationality when emotions may be part of the solution or the problem.

I'm not saying that the church manifested all these symptoms, but they are worthy of reflection from a professional, organisational point of view.

Underlying all this, I would like to adapt a quotation from the family therapist, Jane Howard. She stated that 'Families aren't dying. They won't go away until the whole human race does. What they are doing, in flamboyant and dumbfounding ways, is changing their size and their shape and their purpose.' And so it is with the church: it's not going away. It's changing its size, its shape and its purpose. All that has happened has confused us, but it is affecting and changing the culture of the organisation whether we like it or not. Not all are admitting to it. Some are trying to hold on, thinking that God will intervene and wipe away the blemishes not unlike the way people held on to the priest in the movie *Titanic*. This man of power could reverse a fate that was inevitable. If you look at his face, he is more pained than the rest of them.

Others are evaluating the situation and are arriving at differing conclusions. I would say the majority are listening for signs of hope. They are aware that solutions can't be found, but they would like a lot of honesty. They want someone to express the new hope rather than just talk about how tough it has been. They want this new hope to integrate all that has happened into our new ways of being. They don't want it to be glossed over as if it didn't happen. Account must be taken of all the hurt and bad management if trust is to be restored. Mistakes have been made. Have we learned? The only thing that will convince us is action. One of the findings of those who looked after the aftermath of the Hillsborough disaster was that providing practical support is as important in the aftermath of a disaster as the provision of counselling. We must remember that this instance of the church's history has permeated the deepest part of the church's nature. Just as abuse slays the soul and spirit of the person abused, so the soul of the church has been touched and harmed. Our sacramental life is changing radically. Practice is falling. Fewer and fewer priests are on panels on radio and TV shows. There is the threat of going broke because of claims. There is no information as to how many people have sought help, compensation or counselling, or how many have sought help without seeking compensation. And, accompanying all of this is, 'Father knows best' or 'His Lordship knows best', so no one is told. The more complex or chaotic an individual's communication network, the more symptoms of stress are exhibited. Within this we have the added complexity of differing ecclesiologies, and which one is influencing decisions?

Ultimately, people and ministers are looking at this church

that is changing. They are asking themselves, 'Can I commit myself to what I see?' As a priest, loyalty is presumed rather than asked for. One can be loyal to truth but not to secrets. Can I be a part of this new church that has fallen from its previous privileged position? Such questions are seen as a threat rather than an opportunity for dialogue and learning. Within these questions, we are asking for people to have courage to articulate this new vision. We are looking for leadership that will show courage and openness towards the culture that has evolved. When I went for ordination I was told that my responses to God, in terms of my promises, were not made on one day, They would be made every day. I am hungry to say 'Yes', but the food needs to be put on the table.

Part of the solution

I found this part of the statement, which I quoted at the beginning, initially the most confusing, but I have since found it spurred me towards a response. There is a parable told of a man who was placed in a prison, 100 yards long by 100 yards wide. The ceiling was about 18 feet high. There was an opening, one-foot in diameter, through which he was fed. He was told that there was a way out of the cave if he could find it. He spent his first week building up rocks and soil towards the ceiling. He could almost reach the ceiling if he jumped, but he was so weak he couldn't make it. One day he thought he could touch the opening. He jumped, fell and was too weak to get up. He died two days later. When the stone that covered the entrance was rolled across, one could see a three-foot round tunnel at the back of the cave. If he had searched the walls he would have found it. He was so focused on the light that it never occurred to him to look for freedom in the darkness. Liberation was at hand, but it was in the darkness.

As carers, we are so comfortable with other people's darkness. We can stand back from situations and show wonderful care; we can think rationally and logically. But what of our own darkness and chaos? Who looks after it? To whom do we bring it? In the caring professions, or in priesthood, there can be a macho element whose ethos is 'Get on with the work.' We should be able to cope with anything that is thrown at us. Looking for support or help is a sign of weakness. If this is not taken account of, those who are helping can become a bigger burden on those they are supposed to be helping

Framing a response
No organisation can solve it's own problems. It can, however, be committed to each individual in such a way that it facilitates a person's well-being. When the Panama Canal was being built the builder met with a lot of problems. Many thousands died and the French abandoned the project. The Americans took over with the help and assistance of a British engineer. After a year he was making too little progress. He ordered all work to be stopped. He spent a fortune on the accommodation and sanitary conditions of the workers. When this task was complete, he fixed his attention on the main project and great headway was made.

One reflection that is arising from the instance of Child Sexual Abuse is that many of the people who abused had been abused themselves. They may not have been physically abused but we know there are many forms of abuse. Abuse continued in their lives, and the organisations of which they are a part continued the abuse. By fixing on sexual abuse we are looking at the ceiling rather than exploring the foundations. We should start by looking at the resources we have in place for our carers and ask are they adequate. There is one organisation that admitted responsibility for the level and depth of hurt that they may have caused others. The characteristic of that organisation now is the charitable and caring way in which it looks after its own, even those that have left.

The path forward is through one's own pain. There are no short-cuts in the journey from victim to survivor. If one hasn't paid attention to the way one has been affected, and tried to resolve the situation, even greater harm may result. The answer is not in textbooks and prayer alone. It is a scandal that there are no Employee Assistance programmes in place for priests and bishops. If a cleric has issues that he needs resolved, he has to do so in a forum that may spill into other agendas. Unless this changes, the problems will be perpetuated. Space that has clearly defined boundaries is needed for a person to search his or her soul. We are responsible people but we need to be supported in our desire to be accountable to our priestly nature, which is made known in our humanity. Another lesson learnt in research from the Hillsborough disaster is that support for the carers should be extra-departmental. Helping agencies that are linked to management structures aren't trusted. Staff are the most valuable asset of any organisation, yet many organisations spend more on inanimate assets than on maintaining the well-being of their staff. In order to deliver a quality service, staff should feel valued and supported. This was the secret that brought about the completion of the Panama Canal.

Conclusion
As an organisation the church should not be afraid of darkness. It was in the darkness of the tomb that the power to overcome all things was granted to the church. The instance of Child Sexual Abuse can be seen as an opportunity for change. The primary change is that nobody should be sexually or physically abused again.

At the heart of this is the effectiveness of people believing in themselves again. What we are called to enable is the transition from victim to survivor, being empowered by belief in oneself. At the level of the individual and the organisation, chaos and disaster ask us to rewrite the script. The challenge is to move from an old worldview to a new worldview. That transition involves recognising the chaos, absorbing and releasing the shock, taking account of self-destructive choices that one may make in the process, seeing the gifts that are emerging, following new energy that emerges and allowing it form a creative base that will give a new worldview that will allow the mission of the church to continue. Paul VI, in the preparation of *Gaudium et Spes* (With Joy and Hope), said the objective was to provide principles rather than solutions, direction rather than directives, leaving priests and laity free but not free floating.

The Dilemma of those in Authority

Bishop Colm O'Reilly

In media training sessions there is often a slot for the 'ambush interview'. Participants are asked to respond to a question without any forewarning of its subject matter. Asked to say a few words about Child Sexual Abuse in these circumstances, a person in my position would have no problem in stringing a few words together. The problem would be to avoid going on for twenty minutes instead of an allotted three. We know so much, in a sense. And yet in another way it all remains baffling. It is also surely a depressing topic. We all deep down long for it to be just some kind of passing nightmare. But this will not go away, ever, it seems.

My brief is to deal with the problem from my own perspective as bishop. The professional angles are matters to be covered by others. I shall be concentrating on the pastoral role of the bishop while keeping an eye on the legal issues that bishops and superiors cannot ignore.

Out of denial
First let me make a few general points that must be addressed. The strange and sad phenomenon which is Child Sexual Abuse is not a product of these times. It is evidence of what is referred to sometimes as the shadow side of our humanity, the dark side of sexuality and, some would say, power out of control. The fact that this matter has come to the fore has to be good in the long run. For all the pain that we have suffered in this last few years, it is good that this matter has been exposed, named and addressed. Victims have been thereby given hope and others spared their fate. It seems to me to be important that bishops should say this.

Secondly, the tendency to drift into denial is not a matter confined to offenders only. People like me can do so. We can pretend that offenders are not really from our own world. And one of the hardest things to accept is that the offender is generally unrecognisable from his peers. Denial can also take the form of demonisation. And we do a lot of this in these times. One common expression of it is, I believe, what we call 'road rage'. By attacking speedsters, verbally or mentally, we exonerate ourselves. Bishops as well as drivers must not take refuge in denial!

Thirdly, let me acknowledge that it has been difficult for us to avoid being defensive. It is natural, or maybe I should say second nature to us, to be defensive. We hold certain values dear and who would blame us for wanting to safeguard them? We lived in a culture where it was deemed to be totally normal for a bishop to defend a priest and protect him, almost whatever the situation was.

I confess that I was in disbelief when I first heard outlined, at a Seminar in Cork, a catalogue of crimes committed by clergy. The presenter was speaking about his experience in an institute where clergy of all denominations were being treated. I was convinced that the like of what he described just could not be true of the priests I knew. But now I know that what we heard at that Seminar was exactly the same as the scenario which would unfold in our own country and in our own church.

When the horror of the Brendan Smyth cases hit the headlines we all knew things would never be the same again. My own response at that time was to write a letter to the priests and I also wrote one to be read to the people. I said I was distressed. I said I was apologising for the crimes committed. I encouraged anyone with a need to be heard to come forward.

Reactions varied. Some priests found the letter too difficult to read. I have reason to believe that some people got courage at that time to come forward and speak about matters which had troubled them for decades. Some people were saddened and disappointed that I wrote the letter at all, and told me so. And at that time I did not know if I had done the correct thing, and I agonised a great deal about it. I do not want to whinge about the pain which was involved, but I think it is fair to say that when Cardinal Daly said at the time that he shed tears, he spoke for many people as well as himself.

When I hear people speak in any context of the long journey from the head to the heart, I continue to think of what that journey has meant for people who have had to deal with abusers at first hand. At this stage, most of us know priests and religious who have been found guilty of terrible crimes against children. We must not think that the fact that they have been accused or convicted is the worst news. The worst is that they offended and that innocent people were hurt.

The bishop, a pastor of all his people
If I were asked to put in one sentence the greatest challenge facing a bishop in relation to Child Sexual Abuse, I would say that it is: to hold in balance the responsibilities which are in apparent conflict with each other. Compare the situation of lawyers and bishops here. A lawyer defending an accused person has a simple agenda: protect him at all costs. His counterpart acting for the victim will, of course, be doing the very same thing for the person who is his client. But the bishop has pastoral responsibility for all. The bishop cannot choose his side.

Now let me refer to the document which is entitled *Child Sexual Abuse: Framework for a Church Response.*[1] (hereafter referred to as the framework document). Let me say that we owe an enormous debt of gratitude to the people who were responsible for putting this document together. It may not be, and is not, I expect, perfect in all respects. But it provides a well ordered set of protective supports and ensures, insofar as this is possible at the present time, that bishops are freed up to fulfil their pastoral role. As I want to emphasise later, the bishop must listen and respond to both complainants and accused with real empathy, while still keeping a watchful eye on legal issues and responsibilities.

Before the arrival of the framework document, dreadful mistakes were made by bishops and superiors because they were so frightened of the law that they were rendered unable to actually listen to people. And sometimes our responses in the early days have begun to look very badly in the light of more balanced understanding of priorities now. But I do believe we are all likely to do much better nowadays. We have been able, I believe, at last to give better quality attention to complainants, directly or through our delegates. And we would not underestimate the need to take care of the accused. And, as I say all this, I am also very conscious that the primary concern at all times is the protection of children. And, while saying this, I would not want it in any way to be understood as diminishing the importance of other aspects of our care.

The demands of caring
I think it might be helpful at this point if we tried to imagine the situation faced by a bishop as he sits down with the complainant or accused. Let us take the complainant first. The delegate[2] has a key role in all of the initial dialogue, of course. But I believe it is very desirable that the bishop should meet with the complainant and should even make the offer to do so.

As I sit opposite somebody who has made a complaint or is making one for the first time, I must be conscious of what is in the mind of the person before me. All the experts say that the first need of a complainant is to be believed. So the person is likely to think in her mind, 'Will the bishop actually believe what I am saying?' The complainant is also quite likely to be thinking, 'He will take the side of the priest.' And I believe it is also likely that the complainant may be thinking, 'He will be interested in the law and he will be anxious to protect both the priest and himself.'

So what is the bishop thinking meantime? Well I believe the first essential is that he must keep an open mind. The person who is sitting in front of him is most likely to be telling the truth. All the experts tell us that, in the vast majority of cases, complaints are well founded. But some are not, as have been proven.

And the bishop has to keep in mind at all times that the priest whose name is mentioned is innocent in the eyes of canon and civil law. Nothing has been proved. All that exists is an allegation.

So the question is: How does the bishop meet the first need of the complainant, the need to be believed? Well, the only answer I can give to this is that the bishop must welcome the person who has come, he must thank her for coming forward and he must promise to take every word that she has spoken seriously. I think if all that is said it will go some distance towards reassuring the complainant.

When it comes to his meeting with the priest, the concerns of the bishop are different. He tells the priest that an allegation has been made and 'that it is being dealt with in accordance with the procedure of the diocese'. What is going through the mind of the priest about whom the allegation has been made at this stage? I believe that one of the questions in his mind will surely be, 'Will the Bishop stand by me?' The framework document has the following sentence which indicates to the bishop that he should offer reassurance to the priest: 'The bishop should assure the accused person of his availability and pastoral concern, which would also extend to the members of the accused person's family.' I do not know exactly how individual bishops would phrase this, but I would tend to say that I am truly sorry that this matter has come up and that I want to assure the priest in front of me that I will continue to be his friend. It would be dangerous, to say the least, if he were to leave the room feeling that the bishop had changed his relationship with him and was now simply concerned with canon and civil law issues.

Let us take a look at the wider group of people affected by the arrival of an allegation. The framework document makes mention of many kinds of victims. All of them fall within the general category of people for whom the bishop must have a pastoral concern. The victims' families are also victims. These include parents, brothers and sisters, possibly the spouse and children of somebody who is now an adult. The priest's family and friends, whom I have just mentioned, are also victims. So too, to a certain extent, are parishioners, past or present, to whom he has ministered. And the victims include his fellow priests. It is a lengthy list and yet all of these people somehow must be considered when we talk about the pastoral care to be provided for all by the bishop.

The framework document provides for supports for the accused priest and for the victim. The priest adviser and the victim support person can be people of great importance in the early days after an allegation comes. But let me add that the bishop can do no more than to try as best he can to make sure that these are accessible. If either the accused or the victim chooses not to avail of the help offered, there is little enough that the bishop can do to assist in this particular way.

Lastly, let me say that the framework document does provide a very good system and provides guidance from the moment an allegation comes, right through to the aftermath of investigation, possible conviction, etc. But there is one important thing that bishops and superiors must not forget. Each and every case is unique. There is no precise way in which one can tell a person how to handle any one of the allegations that comes his way. Tolstoy said that 'each unhappy family is unhappy in its own unique way'. Sadly, every story of abuse is also unhappy in its own deeply sad and unique fashion.

Notes:
1. *Child Sexual Abuse: Framework for a Church Response,* Bishops of Ireland, Dublin: Veritas, 1996.
2. Ibid.

Forgiveness and Reconciliation in the Context of Child Sexual Abuse

Eugene Duffy

Introduction

When one talks of healing, forgiveness and reconciliation in the context of Child Sexual Abuse, one is moving in a highly emotive area. We are still dealing with an area of experience that has only in very recent times come to public prominence and awareness. In preparing this paper, I looked at what was one of the most enlightened moral theology text books in the eighties, *Free and Faithful in Christ,* written by Bernard Häring in 1981.[1] It dealt with the ethics of topical issues such as ecology and information technology but it contained no mention of Child Sexual Abuse. It mentioned various kinds of sexual deviance, including masochism, sadism, fetishism and bestiality, but did not mention Child Sexual Abuse. Thus one has to conclude that, even in very enlightened areas of moral discourse, Child Sexual Abuse is a relative newcomer. This, however, is not to suggest that it is a new phenomenon. Rather, the changes in culture and particularly, I suspect, the development of feminism, have created the conditions in which this painful and destructive issue can be spoken about with some degree of freedom. Since it is such a relatively new subject of discourse, none of us is yet entirely comfortable dealing with it or speaking of it.

This unease is reflected in the public coverage which the issue receives in the media. One of the tabloid papers, recently, had sensational headlines following the conviction of a Christian Brother for child sexual abuse. It read: '5 Year Hell at Hands of Pervert Cleric'. We all remember the headlines following the conviction of Brendan Smith: 'Rot in Hell', and the sinister looking man who was shown grimacing at the cameras as he was led from the courtroom. This sensationalised approach to the issue is a reflection of the deep anger that is caused when people realise that vulnerable and innocent people have been abused by those in whom they should have been able to place their trust and confidence. There is the realisation that power has been abused and serious violence done to the weak and vulnerable. Inevitably, too, it taps into the very ambiguity of all our own sexual energies and our potentialities for abusing our own power in relationships. These possibilities which are within ourselves are not yet well explored and so their ambiguities generate fear of ourselves, which can be directed outwards in anger towards others who may be seen to act out our own worst fears about ourselves.

The reality is that we are dealing with a relatively new phenomenon in our discourse and so there is a certain inevitability that sensationalised ideas and information are in possession. If there is to be any talk of healing, reconciliation and forgiveness, then these must be situated in the context of truth and informed discussion. In the first paper, Attracta Shields explored the most recent research that is available in this area. One of the significant issues that she raised was the importance of understanding Child Sexual Abuse in the context of the systemic factors which contribute to its emergence. Child Sexual Abuse can also be viewed in some instances as a serious psychological pathology. Just as one must attempt to understand the pathology of those who abuse, one must also try to have a better grasp of the effects which this abuse has on the survivors. Here, too, there are degrees of damage and recovery. On both sides of the issue we need to continue to be better informed than we are at the moment. We have a serious responsibility to keep ourselves as informed as we can on the best contemporary research. At the same time, even that research will always have a provisional character and so there is a need for a genuine openness to new information and new insights as we try to get to the truth of this issue.

Forgiveness and the survivor
It is far too easy to focus on instant forgiveness and to expect

that those who have suffered abuse can easily forgive and forget. For people who are involved in ministry this can be a first temptation because the Christian message is so strong on the importance of forgiveness and reconciliation. It is indeed an important part of the Christian response to injustices perpetrated against us, but there must be a serious recognition that forgiveness and reconciliation are a long process and, in the end, a gift from God, not something which we can easily manipulate. We can be Pelagian in our approach and say 'you should' or 'I must forgive and be reconciled', forgetting that God gives the gifts we need in God's time and these come through a process of healing and prayer.

On the negative side, it is important to be aware that urging someone to instant forgiveness can be a sign of our own discomfort with the anger and grief of the survivor. It can be a form of denial and a means of suppressing our own feelings or avoiding having to deal with them. Genuine forgiveness must allow the truth to emerge, with all its pain, its anger and grief. As we read in chapter three, it is very important that there is someone there who is prepared to listen attentively and non-judgmentally to the story that the survivor has to tell. This process can not be short-circuited and it may take a very long time for the whole truth to be told and acknowledged. The person, then, has to be helped to work through all the pain, fear, anger, powerlessness and even feelings of guilt which may be associated with the past experiences. Forgiveness would be premature if these stages of the process are not acknowledged and the person allowed the opportunity to integrate these into the whole of her or his life. Somehow, the person has to have the time and space to get in touch with his or her own strength, power and beauty.

Part of the process of healing and forgiveness for the survivor must be self-forgiveness. Because Child Sexual Abuse has been such a taboo subject, most survivors tend to blame themselves to some extent for what has happened. This can be reinforced by the person who has perpetrated the abuse imputing some responsibility in their direction. The promise of affection and acknowledgement is sometimes easily accepted by those who have been deprived of these important supports in their childhood and, therefore, they can be especially vulnerable to the advances of the someone who is a paedophile. This alone should alert us to the innocence that has been exploited and abused. The task, then, is to enable the person to acquire and develop a sense of his or her own dignity, value and beauty in all their relationships and ultimately in their relationship with God.

Forgiveness can only be forthcoming if the survivors have been able to let go their feelings of shame and guilt, pain, anger and grief. The facilitation of this is a very skilled task and can only be done by someone who is well equipped to undertake it. Obviously the development of psychology and counselling skills play a big part in this process and, from the Christian perspective, these must be viewed as a God-given gift to be used for the good of each person. Whatever enables the person to grow and flourish has to be seen as an instance of God's gracefulness towards humankind. As our survivor's story reminds us, one of the phrases which put her on the road to recovery was that line from an early theologian in the church, which she heard at a talk: 'The glory of God is the human person fully alive.'

Forgiveness and those who abuse
The question of forgiveness for those who have abused is a much more emotive and sensitive issue than is the question for the survivor. In this section I would like to focus on the forgiveness which the community may be called upon to extend to the person responsible for the abuse. The current lack of knowledge about the causes of this kind of behaviour, and the extent to which it has been sensationalised in the media, make a reasonable response all the more difficult.

The language which we use in describing people is something to which we have become much more sensitive and this is good because it raises our awareness of the person's dignity. So, for instance, we do not talk about the mentally handicapped, we talk of *people* with a mental handicap. We put the emphasis on the uniqueness of the person, not on their disability. Similarly, I think we need to speak of people who have abused, rather than of abusers or perpetrators. One of the strengths of the Christian tradition is that it can distinguish the sinner from the sin. Therefore, I suggest that we have to begin by acknowledging the dignity of the person who has sexually abused others and make some effort to understand where he or she may be coming from and how his or her background has in some way conditioned the abusive behaviour.

Our knowledge gleaned from psychology and psychiatry with regard to Child Sexual Abuse is still at an early stage. However, there is evidence to suggest that a person's predisposition to commit these offences can have roots in chemical imbalances in the brain, or in the fact that they may have been exposed to privation, violence or abuse in their own childhood. There is also another social factor which may contribute to the fact that more men seem to abuse than women. The fact is that men are more socialised and conditioned to exercise power and strength than women and, therefore, their exercise of power and violence has culturally, perhaps, been more accepted than should be the case. A certain acceptance of the dominant male may be one of the contributory factors to abuse not having been spoken of openly until relatively recently. In this context, too, it may be worth noting that those who abuse are usually not strangers on the rampage, but people known to the child or people in positions of recognised trust and responsibility – fathers, uncles, other relatives, clergy, teachers, healthcare personnel and sports coaches. For the most part, those who abuse are not a foreign breed seeking those whom they can abuse; rather they are among those whom we know and trust.

The French have a proverb which says that to understand all is to forgive all. I am not here arguing for any cheap grace, but I am suggesting that our understanding of why people abuse their power in acts of sexual violence on others needs more development. A better understanding of the reasons which trigger the abusive behaviour will not diminish the pain and the damage to those who have been abused, but it may make us less ready to condemn harshly the person who has inflicted such harm on them.

Of course, people who abuse need to be brought face to face with the reality of their offences. They have to be helped to name the wrong which they have done because forgiveness depends, too, on the person appreciating his or her own need for forgiveness and reconciliation. St Luke, the most compassionate evangelist says, 'If your brother does something wrong, reprove him and, if he is sorry, forgive him' (17:3). Repentance is no lighthearted matter in the scriptures; it involves a desire to change one's attitude, accompanied by steps that lead to a change of behaviour. Unless a person has some appreciation of the seriousness of what they have done they will not even hear the word of forgiveness.

A concept which used to be strong in the Catholic tradition was restitution. If you stole something from another you were expected to make restitution before forgiveness was complete. In the case of Child Sexual Abuse it may be worth considering that those who have been responsible for the abuse should be expected to make some restitution by way of paying for counselling and therapy for their victims where this is possible. It may be a much more important and valuable approach than the purely punitive one to which we have had exclusive recourse up to this point.

Our ineptitude, at present, in dealing with Child Sexual Abuse was highlighted in the contrasting funeral liturgies of Brendan O'Donnell and Brendan Smith. It was quite clear that O'Donnell had severe psychiatric problems which had arisen from a variety of sources, not least his own familial background. He committed very serious crimes – violently killing a mother, her child and a priest. When he died the bishop and some priests from the diocese of Clonfert, where the crimes had been committed, attended the funeral and, on behalf of the victims, spoke words of healing and forgiveness. This could happen, I suspect, because people knew that this young man was seriously disturbed and could not be held totally responsible in any normal way for the enormity of his crime.

When Smith died, the obsequies were carried out in the middle of the night under the lights of a digger. There were no bishops or visiting clergy present. This man, too, had committed enormous crimes and a very significant number of people have been seriously damaged by what he did to them. However, there did not seem to be any understanding of the fact that this man, too, was indeed a seriously sick man. If we could acknowledge that, then our response could be more mature and constructive.

Those who commit sexual abuse against children are the contemporary lepers in our society. They are to be kept outside the city gates. They can easily become the scapegoats for all kinds of sexual deviance in our midst; Child Sexual Abuse is judged to be the worst form of deviance and therefore our abhorrence of any kind of sexual deviance is directed against this group. This is true within the prison community too, which is merely a microcosm of the wider society. It seems to be acceptable that their concessions within the prison system are even more limited than those serving sentences for any other category of crime. They are imprisoned and without any realistic treatment to address their condition. This is a serious issue. There is evidence that treatment does have a positive outcome in very many situations. There is no doubt that the resources which would be required to provide adequate treatment would be an enormous financial burden to society, but the question has to be asked: does capital have priority over the person? The cost must surely act as a deterrent for attempting a genuinely humane response to this problem. On the other hand, it is hard to see what treatment could work out as any more costly than the current costs of imprisonment in this country.

It cannot be denied that there is also another even more serious responsibility on the state, namely, to protect those who are vulnerable and who may be at risk from people who may abuse them. However, in general the most serious risks come from within families and relationships of trust and responsibility, not, for the most part, from strangers on the loose. Therefore it seems unlikely that the state can ever adequately protect those who are at risk of being sexually abused.

Challenges for the church
Child Sexual Abuse is a real problem for the church to deal with, especially among those who hold positions of responsibility. The church in the past described itself as the perfect society. Although it no longer does so, it understands itself to be a community guided by the Holy Spirit, the sacrament of salvation, a genuinely holy people. Therefore, to have to admit serious crime and sinfulness in the very heart of this community is particularly painful, and so the natural tendency is either towards denial or over zealous reaction once the evil has been exposed. This is compounded further by a theology of priesthood which speaks of ontological change effected by ordination, a change which cannot be reversed by any human power. This tends to put the priest into another category of being apart from the ordinary baptised member of the church. It makes accountability and dismissal difficult. Thus one can see that, for church authorities dealing with this issue, not only are there all the difficulties that others in society have to cope with, but they also have to struggle with theological considerations which may act as inhibiting factors.

Here, perhaps there is a new opportunity for a prophetic response to a serious social problem, one which will respect the dignity of those who have abused, on the one hand, and on the other, one which will protect the vulnerable, the weak and those at risk. Is it possible that some new form of community could be created where these people who have abused could find a home, with proper therapeutic facilities, proper supervision and the opportunity, when and as appropriate, to be reintegrated into a normal living situation, where their weakness is acknowledged, without having to be treated in purely punitive fashion? In this way their dignity could be restored and honoured, as Christ always seemed to do with the sinner and, at the same time, the concerns of the wider society would be safeguarded. The challenge to stand with the public sinner is never an easy one, yet it is the great paradox of the sinless Jesus that he was himself condemned for his socialising with the public sinners of his time, including those guilty of sexual deviance. Our forgiveness cannot be confined to the privacy of the confessional, where the hidden sins are absolved, even the most heinous of crimes. It is important for us to remember that God loves all sinners, those whose sins are public just as much as those whose sins remain private and unknown.

Notes:
1. *Free and Faithful in Christ,* Vol III, Middlegreen, Slough: St Paul Publications, 1981.

The Service of a Different Kingdom: Child Sexual Abuse and the Response of the Church

Eamonn Conway

Introduction
This paper sets out to explore theologically some aspects of the recent Irish experience of child sexual abuse by priests and religious and to assess the implications for the life and ministry of the church.

The insights of psychologists, of lawyers and of other professionals are indispensable to the church at this time. But the church is not like any other body in society. The church has a unique mandate to proclaim God's unconditional love, to embody it and to model this love for all of humankind. When church personnel abuse children, something has gone drastically wrong, and it strikes at the very nature of the church. It is my contention that only a theological reflection, in dialogue with the work of psychologists and the experience of counsellors, can unpack fully the significance of recent events for the mission of the church.

This paper attempts such a theological reflection. The first part will take up comments by people who have worked with victims and offenders and suggest some implications for the church's self-understanding and for society as a whole. The second part will re-visit the core message of Christianity and in that light suggest that the experience both of victims of sexual abuse and sexual offenders needs to be listened to by the church if it is to fulfil its mission at this challenging time.

Sexual abuse and dominative power
Olive Travers, in her book *Behind the Silhouettes,* argues that sexual abuse is often as much about control and power as it is about

sex; that the control which sex offenders exercise over their victims serves as a compensation for the powerlessness they feel in relationships with other adults.[1] Non-fixated offenders, and most priests and religious who abuse belong in this category, usually perceive themselves as powerless. At the same time, they can hold rigid views about the traditional roles of men and women in society.[2]

Marie Keenan, a psychotherapist with the Granada Institute, Dublin, believes that power imbalances in society are part of the culture that allows sexual abuse to thrive.[3] Specifically with regard to clergy who have offended, she has commented that few of them are sexual deviants as such. However, they have had great difficulty in dealing with their sexuality and with holding positions of power:

> Where they (clergy) come off the page in assessment is in terms of sexual conflict and uncontrolled hostility ... a tiny minority of abusive priests had a psychologically deviant profile but many had great difficulty in dealing with their sexuality or dealing with having positions of power and yet a feeling of no power over their own lives.[4]

The English Benedictine, Sebastian Moore, also discusses the relationship between clergy sexual misconduct and the exercise of power. In a recent collection of essays published to honour his eightieth birthday, Moore writes:

> Celibate priesthood is extraordinarily symptomatic of the arrested condition of the Western male. We are the sons of Mother Church, our phallic energy exiled in obedience to her command. Our history shows, especially in the higher echelons of the priesthood, the resultant transformation of phallic energy into dominative power. And now our order is manifesting, to an embarrassing degree, the symptoms of denial, of resistance to the change which is being demanded of man generally ... as dioceses are bankrupting themselves with lawsuits over our sexual irregularities ...[5]

Moore situates the relatively small number of sexual misconduct cases by clergy within the wider context of abuse of power in the church. Western culture, according to Moore, has been characterised by this need among men to dominate, and the church, far from challenging this tendency, is in danger of being the last bastion of it in Western society.[6]

Some may hold that male sexual energy and dominative power find symbolic expression in spires and obelisks, but there are more serious examples to be considered which have done immense damage to the mission and ministry of the church. Mention must be made straight away of the deliberate and persistent exclusion of women from any decision-making or authoritative leadership role in the church. There are other examples:

- The persistence of a hierarchical model of authority and of decision-making;
- The desire to hold on to authority positions late into life;
- The reluctance of priests to share decisions with laity and even with fellow-priests (as this becomes increasingly embarrassing, there is some reluctant acceptance of the need for 'consultation');
- A theology of sacraments which emphasises the 'power of the priest' and what only he can 'do';
- Attitudes to the charism of celibacy: arguments in favour of it being obligatory for priests; the opinion that it is a superior state to that of marriage;
- Images of God which are male, authoritarian and judgmental;
- A preoccupation with titles and honours;
- The many different bachelor shields, from a preoccupation with computers to fast cars.

The 'still arrested condition of the Western male', as Moore puts it, also finds expression in certain kinds of devotions to the Blessed Virgin Mary. Surely it is no coincidence that some of the most rigid of Catholic clerics have an almost fanatical devotion to the Virgin-Mother of God?[7]

The psychological evidence referred to earlier would seem to suggest that few clerical sexual offenders are technically sexual deviants. It would seem, however, that frequently their abuse of children has to do with power and control, and their inability to resolve such issues in a mature way. There are many instances of the abuse of power and control by priests and religious other than sexual abuse. For the most part, these abuses are not illegal and therefore do not lead to criminal charges. However, in terms of the church's self-understanding, these are no less wrong and sinful. In terms of the church's unique mission to the world, they are no less dimming of the light the church is called to be, in the darkness of everyday exploitation, injustice, and violation of human dignity.

It is remarkable that the revelation of abuse, both physical and sexual, by priests and religious has been like music to the ears of so many people, including practising Catholics. The sad reality is that while few experienced this kind of abuse themselves, many experienced other kinds of abuse of power by authorities in the church. When many Catholics hear about cases of abuse, I believe that in their own minds, perhaps unconsciously, they connect these stories with their own memories of abuse and hurt by clerics. These memories have never found expression until now. The cases of Child Sexual Abuse may have become a vehicle for the expression of a wider experience of the abuse of church power.

The reaction so far: scapegoating
There is a tendency in the media to make sexual offenders seem as unlike the ordinary person as possible. But as Travers notes, 'sex offenders are just like us. We all have the potential within us to abuse ... All of us are abusive in our relationships to some degree. We lose our tempers with children, we use our power over them, we let our moods determine their treatment.'[8] The response has been to distance us as far as possible from sexual offenders. Cameras in slow motion and graphic headlines attempt to portray abusers as a subhuman species. Society demands lengthy prison sentences as punishment. Within prison, sexual offenders must be segregated from 'ordinary decent criminals'. On release, no community wants them. There are calls for the regist-

ration and/or the tagging of sex offenders, the twenty-first century equivalent of 'branding', a practice most societies would now consider barbaric.

It is superficial to see these responses as motivated only by a concern for the sensibilities of victims or the protection of children.[9] The truth is that sexual offenders are a painful reminder to all of us of our own potential to abuse and hurt others, especially in areas of sexuality and relationships. By distancing ourselves from sexual offenders, we can distance ourselves from that part of us which we do not even wish to acknowledge. Travers refers to this as scapegoating. Scapegoating, according to the cultural theorist René Girard, is the most primitive means of restoring order and harmony in a community.[10]

Since the beginning of time, communities have been establishing themselves 'over against' individuals whom they have identified as a threat. Community is formed or re-formed in working together to defeat a common enemy; unlikely alliances are forged and potentially divisive squabbles are resolved or left aside. When the perceived enemy has been defeated and expelled, and when harmony is restored to the community, the community finds it is in a better state than before. It is then presumed that all the ills which beset the community were in fact the fault of the individual now expelled and that it is his/her defeat and expulsion which has brought about the new spirit of co-operation and understanding.

This concept of scapegoating explains some of the reaction to sexual offenders in contemporary Irish society and in the media. First of all, sexual offenders serve as scapegoats for our general discomfort with our sexuality. In Ireland, within a few short years, we have gone from being a society within which even mature discussion of sex was taboo, to one which not only condones but also actively encourages all sexual activity so long as consent is given. Every day of the week, sexuality is violated and exploited in the interests of the market and the media. The images, which titillate us all, whether in tabloids or on television or in films, create an environment which supports sexual violation and exploitation. They lead us to think that all our sexual dreams and fantasies can be satisfied, and that we have a right to satisfy them. They caricature any form of conscience with regard to sexuality.

At some deep place in ourselves we know that sexuality is precious and sacred. Yet we rarely challenge the popular sexual discourse and images. It is reassuring, therefore, to have a clearly labelled class of people called 'sexual offenders' over against whom we can assure ourselves of our own sexual propriety. Sex offenders are those whose sexual lives are out of control. The rest of us are ok.

Sex offenders must take full responsibility for their crimes. They are guilty of horrific violations of human dignity. At the same time, however, they may be innocent of much for which society punishes them. It is no more their fault than it is ours that we live in a society in which sex is the most marketable of commodities. It is not their fault that we live in a society which is sexually immature, in which many people are frightened of their sexuality, and find it difficult to express it in ways that build relationships and give life in every sense of the term. It is not their fault that we live in a society which, despite the prosperity of some, leaves many of its citizens disempowered and with a sense of helplessness, which is in turn compensated for by a variety of forms of addiction. It is not their fault that public attitudes make it very difficult for people in trouble with their sexuality to seek help. Lastly, it is not their fault that there is so little help available for the few who have the courage to seek it.

At some level we know all this, and occasionally we feel guilty about it. But the existence of a clearly labelled category of criminals makes it easier for us to run away from the criminal neglect in which we all share as members of society.

The church can scapegoat offenders too
Turning to the reaction within the church, we find that many priests and religious, including those in leadership, have shown great compassion and understanding towards colleagues con-

victed of sexual abuse. Their capacity to cope with a colleague who has offended has been determined by their own level of self-knowledge and self-acceptance. Many have realised that 'but for the grace of God' it could be them. Some, while journeying with imprisoned colleagues, have heard the call to travel a painful road of personal reflection themselves, reviewing their own sexuality and how it finds celibate expression.

Bishops and congregational leaders genuinely have been torn in their efforts to be compassionate and, at the same time, pastorally responsible to victim and offender. At one level, the protection of children, legal considerations, and the public demand for justice has determined church policy. At a deeper level, however, there are signs of scapegoating within the church as well, signs that it has been considered better 'to have one man die for the people than to have the whole nation destroyed'.[11] As Girard notes, expulsion is always unifying. It restores order and harmony to the community. It enables the flock to believe it is 'pure' again. It encourages the view that while there may have been one or two 'rotten apples', the barrel itself is sound. The permanent exclusion from active ministry of priests and religious who have been convicted of sexual offences allows us to believe that with it, all clerical problems have been resolved and that we can get back to business as usual. The clerical caste, as such, remains intact and deeper questions need not be asked. We need not ask, for example, how much energy and resources we have invested in the on-going care and support of priests. We need not raise questions about the kind of structures of organisation that are in place and whether or not they permit or encourage priests and religious to relate and behave in a mature manner. And we can dismiss as irrelevant questions about the appropriateness of a highly authoritarian, exclusively male celibate style of leadership.

Psychologists and prison officials call repeatedly for society to move beyond the dynamic of scapegoating. They urge us all to reflect on our shared culpability with regard to sexual crime.[12] They actively seek a role for communities in responding to offenders and for a shift from retributive to restorative models of justice. The church needs to put its full weight behind such calls. As we shall now go on to see, such calls are precisely in accord with gospel principles. However, the church is in a weak position to support these worthwhile demands unless it is itself prepared to implement them within its own ranks.

Jesus Christ and forgiveness of enemies
A close examination of the significance of the life, death and resurrection of Jesus Christ shows that, *in principle,* the church is well placed to call people out of their instinctive reaction to sexual abuse into a response which promotes healing and which upholds the dignity both of victim and offender. In order to appreciate this, we must take a fresh look at Jesus as portrayed in the gospels.[13]

Jesus made it possible for all people to understand that God's unlimited graciousness was the most original and firm basis for human relationships. However, as a race we had 'fallen' into a different, damaging and destructive manner of being in the world. Instead of relying for our identity on the fact that we were creatures of a gracious God, we felt we had status only when others considered us to be important. We sought security not in God's fidelity to us but in the fact that we owned or possessed more than other people did. Our sense of our own goodness depended on us defining others as less good than ourselves. We were united to people not by the realisation that we were all brothers and sisters, but because we found some other people whom we considered our common enemies. We emphasised their otherness and we confirmed our shared identity by defining ourselves over against them. Violence against other people became acceptable as a way of defending our place in the world and of holding on to our sense of dignity and well-being. When someone hurt us, we came to believe that we had to hit back or else we would be seen as weak.

Scapegoating became an acceptable and even necessary way of achieving social order and harmony. Hebrew religion had, for centuries, made use of an actual scapegoat upon whom the sins of the people were periodically unburdened and who was then driven out into the desert. The evil was thus understood to be removed from people's midst. But this ritual practice was only a reflection of what was happening every day: adulteresses were stoned, demoniacs banished, tax collectors ostracised, lepers outcast, and sinners were considered excluded from both God's company and that of decent people.

Jesus stepped right into the middle of this way of being in the world and called for a total halt to it. He said:

You have heard that it was said, 'An eye for an eye and a tooth for a tooth.' But I say to you, do not resist an evildoer. But if anyone strikes you on the right cheek, turn the other also; and if anyone wants to sue you and take your coat, give your cloak as well; and if anyone forces you to go one mile, go also the second mile. Give to everyone who begs from you, and do not refuse anyone who wants to borrow from you ... You have heard that it was said, 'You shall love your neighbour and hate your enemy.' But I say to you, love your enemies and pray for those who persecute you, so that you may be children of your Father in heaven; for he makes his sun rise on the evil and on the good, and sends rain on the righteous and on the unrighteous.[14]

When we read this text, our first reaction might be that it requires people to accept violence and abuse as their lot, to 'put up' with it, hoping that somehow in the end God will make it up to them. This and other texts have been so interpreted in the past. But that was not the meaning or the intention of Jesus. On the contrary, Jesus is calling people to take the most radical and powerful stand that is possible against violence by refusing to allow themselves to be drawn into it by those who violate or abuse them.

Jesus called for a new basis for human relationships. In the end he offered his life as that basis. If people needed a victim to be the source of unity with one another, then he was prepared to be that victim. Jesus very deliberately stepped outside the cycle of violence and he showed that people are most fully human, most fully themselves, when they do what he did. God's resurrection of Jesus completes the story. Faced with the gravest provocation of all, the murder of God's own son, God still refuses to be drawn into the reciprocity of violence but responds instead with the ultimate gesture of love, the resurrection of Jesus and the gift of eternal life for all, which it signifies.

What Jesus wanted was for all people, whether rich or poor, to be truly free. And the path to true freedom was paved only with God's unconditional love. As long as we depend on the approval of others for our sense of well-being, we are not free. As long as we need to see others as bad so that we can feel good about ourselves, we are not free. As long as we allow the behaviour of others towards us, whether benevolent or hostile, to determine the extent of our graciousness and self-giving, we are not free.

Our *self-giving* is most clearly tested when it comes to the question of *for-giving*. It is at this point that we come most clearly to recognise the fundamental principles by which we have chosen to live our lives. When somebody wrongs us, it might appear that the natural response is to seek revenge, to retaliate. But what Jesus showed is that *this is not the most natural response.* The most original human response, the response that most accords with true human nature, is to forgive. To forgive is to decide that the person who has offended will not define or limit the extent of my graciousness and self-giving. To forgive is to decide that, even in the face of hurt and violation, I will continue to take the risk of giving of myself. To forgive is to decide that I still trust in the power of love to heal and transform, and this despite the horrible violation and hurt that has occurred.

I can only forgive if I do not depend on the 'putting down' of the person who has wronged me in order that I can stand up straight again. I can only forgive if I know that I do not need the wrongdoer's pain in order to feel good about myself. The only thing that can ultimately heal me is the conviction that I am loved exactly as I am and that this love for me is the only thing that matters. If I believe this, then I *must* forgive in order to be true to this love and true to my deepest self. Anything short of forgiveness is allowing the wrongdoer to have the last word regarding the extent of my self-giving.

Sexual abuse is possibly the most difficult of all violations to forgive. Sexuality belongs to that which is most intimate in us. Through our sexuality we can physically express our nature as gracious, self-giving beings. When somebody violates us sexually, they damage this nature. Rape literally means to seize and carry off something. When somebody is raped, it is their capacity to give of themselves which is seized and plundered. The very aspect of their nature by which people enflesh their desire to give of themselves totally, is sacrileged.

It is a moment of breakthrough in terms of healing when victims of horrendous sexual abuse come to forgive those who have violated them. It is also, according to psychologists, a necessary moment in the healing process:

> Anger and lack of forgiveness can keep the adult victim locked in a destructive relationship with her abuser and allow the abuser to continue to ruin their lives. Forgiving does not mean excusing, but it allows the adult to let go of her own crippling anger and resentment and desire to punish her abuser. A rich spiritual life can give adult victims the strength to bear the pain of what has been done to them and to rebuild their lives.[15]

What Christianity has to offer is precisely that conviction at which victims of sexual abuse most need to arrive. It is the conviction that I am loved exactly as I am, and that my deepest self is held in being by God's love for me. By remembering this love I am able to forgive my enemies by acting towards them in a way that is gratuitous, by breaking out of the cycle of hatred, by refusing to be entrapped within the reciprocity of violence.

Christianity has also something to offer the perpetrators of sexual abuse. To them it says, it is only a superficial part of yourself that you seek to gratify by sexual abuse. You are grasping and seeking after a sense of well-being by overpowering others, by dominating them, by attempting to steal love from them, by forcing them to express bodily an acceptance of you for which you crave. But what you crave in your deepest self, that is unconditional love and acceptance, is already yours as a gift if only you could realise it, and if only you had the courage and the humility to accept it.

It has more to say to the offender. It says, faced with the shame of your sexual abuse of another person, Christianity asks you not to think that this defines you as a person. It is God's love and this alone which defines you, not anything you do, whether good or evil. You cannot shake off this love. It is unconditional. When you realise fully the enormity of what you have done you may be tempted to despair. Your sense of self-worth may have been totally eroded by a sense of self-hatred. It is at this moment that you, just like your victim, must remember God's love.

God's gratuitous love is always there in our lives. It is not as if something new is added in the face of our sin and need of forgiveness. Forgiveness, rather, is the particular form which God's love takes when faced with the reality of our sin. Sin not only sunders our relationships with those against whom we sin. It also sunders our relationship with our deepest selves. When we sin we lose contact with our own goodness. We see only our sin and are tempted to allow ourselves to be defined by it. But God's love offers to restore us to ourselves, to heal us. It as if God says to us, 'I know there is more to you than what you have done. I see that. I want you to see that yourself. I know that there is goodness in you that is deeper and more original than your sinful action. I believe in that goodness. I restore you to it and I want you to live out of it.'

A mission to *the church*

Victims of sexual abuse who arrive at some level of healing, and abusers who come to acknowledge the full significance of their wrongful actions, realise that violence and hatred, revenge and retribution cannot bring them peace. They have reached a vacuum in their humanity that only gratuitous, self-giving and forgiving love can fill. Difficult as it is to believe, many victims of sexual abuse by priests and religious still turn to Christian faith, if not to the church, in order to be healed. They do so because they have plumbed the dark and hidden depths of their humanity. And they know, in the light of their painful journey, that only a God who loves as the God of Christ does, who 'loves humanity at its worst' (Moore), can re-fashion their lives.

These people have a mission to the church. They call the church to recover its own hidden depths in Jesus Christ which have been obscured by centuries of conformity to the very kinds of exercise of power, and sources of status and security, which Christ abhorred. Whether as victims or abusers, these people bear the marks of the worst excesses of the abusive power we are all inclined to wield by virtue of our fallen nature. They more than anyone else know its futility.

According to Pope John Paul II, the church 'needs heralds of the gospel who are experts in humanity, who have penetrated the depths of the human heart'. The church has been sent such heralds from among those who have survived the trauma of sexual abuse, whether as victims or offenders. We are being called to listen to them, to listen to their stories and to listen to what the very occurrence of sexual abuse within the church is saying to us. Disturbed Catholics ask when it all will finish. They long for an end to the revelations and the scandals, the constant undermining in the media. They cannot wait for a bright new chapter in the life of the church. In this paper, I have been suggesting that we have a long distance to go until we reach that new chapter. We have a long and painful path of conversion to travel first, a path that will lead us to re-discover the foundations of the church and to re-examine our way of being in the world in the light of our discoveries. However, until we go down that path, regardless of how correctly we celebrate ritual and cite formulae, 'the Christian faith is not being taught, and the words have been pressed into service of a different kingdom.'[16]

THE RESPONSE OF THE CHURCH 89

Notes:
1. Olive Travers, *Behind the Silhouettes,* Belfast: Blackstaff, 1999, 74.
2. By 'non-fixated' is meant offenders who do not have a primary sexual preference for children but who turn to children for sexual satisfaction to compensate for difficulties in (sexual) relationships with other adults. These offenders are not, strictly speaking, paedophiles (Cf Travers, *Behind the Silhouettes,* 47).
3. Address to the NCPI Conference, Athlone, 26 April 1999.
4. Marie Keenan, quoted in the *Irish Independent,* 26 April 1999.
5. Sebastian Moore, 'The Bedded Axle-Tree', *Jesus Crucified and Risen,* William Loewe and Vernon Gregson (Eds), Minnesota: Liturgical Press, 1998, 218.
6. Moore offers the explanation that the Western male psyche has not advanced beyond a relationship to women that is shaped by the relationship of the young man to his mother. Men first encounter women in the role of son to mother. In this relationship men sense the overwhelming 'natural' superiority of women as mothers and, though they grow up physically, emotionally they are unable to move beyond this first relationship into a partnership of equality. Thus, men seek to subjugate women in an effort to overcome their feelings of inferiority towards them. To compensate for women's 'natural' supremacy, men have developed a 'cultural' pre-eminence. In a state of emotional fixation on the mother, there is no place for male sexual energy, which must find other outlets.
7. Moore is very supportive of an authentic Marian piety. In fact, he sees in the doctrine of the Virginal Birth of Christ a reversal of the usual pattern of (1) woman in society subject to man for status; (2) woman dominates man as son; (3) man still 'son' emotionally, fashions domination through the organs of culture. The Virgin Mary is subject to God alone and therefore does not have to dominate the Son, who in turn does not have to dominate her. Instead, Mother participates in the Son's work of mediating the mystery of redemption.
8. Olive Travers, interviewed in *The Irish Times,* 15 Feb 1999. Cf her book, p. 46.
9. 'Both offenders and victims are members of society and what we have to say about them also applies to us. We have to ask ourselves in what ways we are victims and/or offenders and to what extent we have contributed to the abusive behaviour and twisted thinking which resulted in sexual abuse' (Travers, 90).
10. Cf, for example, *Violence and the Sacred,* London: John Hopkins Press, 1977. Girard's work has been taken up by a number of theologians. Most notable are Raymund Schwager, *Must there be Scapegoats?*

Violence and Redemption in the Bible, San Francisco: Harper & Row, 1987, and James Alison, *The Joy of Being Wrong, Original Sin through Easter Eyes*, New York: Crossroad, 1998.
11. John 11:50.
12. '... we are ourselves either colluding with a society which tolerates abuse or seeking to live in one which discourages abusive relationships at all levels. We need to be less complacent about the media messages which exploit and objectify sexuality' (Travers, 112).
13. Here the author wishes to acknowledge the work of James Alison, *The Joy of Being Wrong, Original Sin through Easter Eyes*, New York: Crossroad, 1998.
14. Matthew 5:38ff.
15. Travers, 105. Speaking at the National Conference of Priests of Ireland Conference on Child Sexual Abuse, May 1998, a law lecturer at NUI Galway, Dr Tom O'Malley, stated that, 'Victims' desire for revenge might not be in the best interest of victims themselves and only prolong their suffering.'
16. Alison, p. 2.

The Western Theological Institute, Galway, Ireland

Vision Statement

The Western Theological Institute is a pioneering theological institute offering an unique interface between theology and the human sciences. Drawing upon the distinctive character and imagination of the West of Ireland, it is committed to providing leadership in church and society by:

- Developing and providing courses accredited at third level with guaranteed academic excellence;
- Providing significant educational opportunities for those interested in exploring fundamental questions regarding Christian faith;
- Designing and implementing innovative programmes for the continuing education of clergy and all those involved in church ministry;
- Exercising a leadership role in contemporary debates both in church and society;
- Modelling participative leadership;
- Researching new forms of ecclesial community with a view to the transformation of parish life;
- Other research and publications.

The Contributors

EAMONN CONWAY DD, is a priest of the Tuam diocese and head of theology and religious studies at Mary Immaculate College, University of Limerick. He is also associate director of the Western Theological Institute, Galway.

EUGENE DUFFY DD, is a priest of the diocese of Achonry and director of the Western Theological Institute, Galway.

COLM HEALY is director of a residential child care centre in the Dublin area.

ALAN HILLIARD is a priest of the diocese of Dublin and works in parish ministry.

COLM O'REILLY is Bishop of Ardagh and Clonmacnoise.

ATTRACTA SHIELDS PHD, is a chartered psychologist and a registered psychotherapist. She is a director of the Western Theological Institute, Galway.